An Guide to Greening It

Everything a Modern Woman needs to know to live an eco-friendly life for better health and a better tomorrow

Stephanie Byng

First Edition

Contact:
Stephanie Byng
babesguide@gmail.com

Cover and interior design by Stephanie Byng
Cover photograph by Fabrice Lerouge; ONOKY collection, Getty Images

ISBN: 1440437130
EAN-13: 9781440437137.
Published by CreateSpace

Contents

Acknowledgements

First, I would like to thank my wonderful and amazing Red Ink Editing Posse. Kateryna Boyce, thank you for encouraging me to speak up and for being there when I needed your help. Nick Faulk, we always seem to bump into each other in the weirdest places. Thank you for your encouragement and dependability. 我祝愿你和平，歡樂和幸福. Renee LeClaire, you are one of those few people who really do light up a room. Thank you for your infectious smile. Nina Ricci you are an inspiration and I thank you for your advice and kind words. Ian Zucker, you rock my socks off! הרבה שמחה, אהבה, שלום לך מאחלת אני פמיניסטית ארוטי מקום.

My husband, Matthew Freeman, I will never forget: butterball, cruising, Curragh Chase, wild berries, Brownie, the pavilion, your cell ringing on March 24th, and the feel of your hand in mine. This is for you. Gra Dilseacht Cairdeas.

Finally, I'd like to thank my mother for always supporting me and being there when others weren't. Seeing you always brightens my day and I will cherish and look back fondly on the times we lived together. I love you.

Introduction

What is an Eco-Babe?
You! You care about environmental and social issues; you work hard and have lots of love in your heart. You are a vibrant, amazing woman; a modern woman whose inner beauty shines through. You are intelligent, sophisticated, independent, savvy and fearless.

This Guide is for You!

You are an intelligent woman, which is why I'm going to give it to you straight. In this book, you will learn not only how the decisions you make affect your health and environment, but also why it matters that you make a change. As you progress through this book, feel proud of every single change you make! From turning off the faucet to buying an organic scarf, you are living a green life. Together we will change the world.

Living green does not have to be tedious and boring. It's an exciting foray into the lifestyle of the future; a future of lush natural fabrics, refreshing essential oils and a planet with abundant healthy ecosystems and clean air. Living green does not have to be all about tree hugging, unless you want it to be. If you're a hair dyeing, manicure-loving, and Manolo-wearing babe, you can be just as green as our deadlocked, yoga-doing, and granola-loving sisters! Living green is not about changing who we are, it about adjusting *how* we are.

I became interested in sustainable living after my senior year of college. Some ideas take a long time to incubate; others jump up and smack you hard in the face. After I graduated college, I found myself overqualified and unemployed. I needed to overhaul my life as the path I had set for my life years ago was unclear and didn't pertain to the person I am today. In the process of redefining myself I explored a healthier and greener lifestyle. I have been a business professional, a student, a wanderer, a wife, a housekeeper, a non-profit professional, an activist, and now I am an author – a path I have imagined since my teens. The quest for the American Dream of affluence, possessions, and promotions has resulted in global environmental devastation, class/gender/race inequality, discontent, and disconnection from the natural world. Modern Western society is driven to use, abuse, and manipulate all in the name of the Good Life. We must waste less, and be less dependent on the consumerism that *is* western patriarchal society[1]. I am drawn to help advance sustainable ways of living from a feminist perspective.

In "The Power and the Promise of Ecological Feminism," Karen Warren explains, "Ecological feminism is the position that there are important connections – historical, experiential, symbolic, theoretical – between the domination of women and the domination of nature[2]." Because women are identified with nature, and nature is considered inferior to Man, women are then considered subordinate to men. Thus men are justified in subordinating women. Therein lies the logic of domination that feminists oppose. This logic of domination, according to Ecofeminists, is used to justify the domination of humans by racial, class or gender lines, as well as the domination of nature. Because the oppression of women and nature are so linked, I believe it is important to study feminist theory and environmental ethic as twins of domination.

With less and less natural environment to preserve, time is running short. I want this book to be a manifestation in eco-ethic and sustainability. I believe every woman deserves the right to express her creativity and sexuality as well as live a lifestyle that is safe for her body, her mind and the environment. My mission is to promote a healthier and more positive attitude about women's bodies through education, advocacy and outreach. This book will shed light on the environmental concerns of today and ways in which we can make small adjustments in our personal lives, which will have huge impacts on the Earth. In addition, the fact that this book exists combats gender oppression and the oppressive conceptual framework of patriarchy. Through research, activism, and writing, I want to bring values and insights to the fields of environmental action and advocacy, and feminist theory to influence ecological sustainability and greener lifestyles among women of today's western world.

After I compiled all this research, I wondered how I could apply this knowledge to my life and my home. Other books on the market seem to be written either for wealthy Cosmo-reading stylistas or barefoot, hard-core environmentalists. But what about us women who don't fit either stereotype, who sit in the middle? What about women who have a tight budget? I have no housekeepers, personal assistants or designer clothes. I am an average woman on a fixed income who shops at Wal-Mart out of necessity rather than desire. I would go to yoga classes if I had the time and money, and I'd get my nails done if I knew I wasn't going to break them soon after. In my frustration over the lack of a book written for me, I committed to writing it myself in-between running my household, applying to graduate school and paying off student loans. I knew there had to be more women like me who are on a budget, but want to live greener, but and just don't know how or where to start.

So I give this to you. I want you to feel proud of your choices and live a lifestyle that reflects your values as well. The fact that you have already purchased this book tells me that you are already aware of the impact you have on the world. You may not know exactly what that impact is, but you do know that you can better it. You are beautiful, amazing and precious, and I am honored that you have chosen to walk this path with me. Together we can do great things.

An Eco-Babes Guide to Greening It is a tool that will help you live sustainably for better health and a cleaner world. You will learn how to smell sweet, look chic, have a sparkling home, and much more, without toxic chemicals and forced child labor. By the time you finish this book, you will be armed with the knowledge necessary to make informed and contentious decisions about your lifestyle.

Babes and Their Bodies is all about cleaning, maintaining, and beautifying our bodies. We will discus the various toxic products we use and their alternative natural products. This section also discusses how to shop for organic products and how to make your own spa quality beauty products. I spotlight green diets in *The Yummy Tummy* and provide recipes so you can try them yourself. Finally, we will discuss sweatshops and fabric in *What Are You Wearing*. You will find helpful resources at the end of each chapter, and the super *Internet Shopping Guide* in the Appendix. The *Internet Shopping Guide* contains links to all products mentioned in the book as well as additional products and resources. If you're looking for quick information, this is the place to go.

Babes at Home is all about detoxing your home. I take you through every room of the house and address the various health and environmental hazards. Here you will find the cleaning guide, which includes product recommendations and even recipes so you can make your own cleaning products. *Composting – Not just for farmers anymore,* will take you step-by-step in setting up your own compost heap, which you can do even if you are an urban babe. This section also includes information on recycling, freecyling and greening your pets.

Babes with Babies discusses diapers, toys, clothes and even furniture for your little ones. I've included *The Lil' Yummy Tummy* for mothers wanting to green their children's diets as well. Be sure to check out the Internet Shopping Guide at the end of the book for everything from slings to baby socks.

Finally, *Babes at Work* is a guide to ways in which you can green your workplace. No matter where you work, you should find ways to not only save the company some money, but also ways to create a healthy and productive work environment as well.

This book also spotlights righteous women-owned and operated businesses that are working hard to run sustainably and provide amazing services for us. It's not easy being a business for and of women, in today's world. That is why it's important to support out sisters who are breaking glass ceilings, rocking boats and shaking foundations. In addition, the book contains tips, tricks and stories from real women about what they do to live a greener life. It is my hope that the stories you read about these businesses and fellow eco-babes will empower and inspire you.

How do I use this book?

I suggest you start at the beginning, as knowledge is built as we go. It's ok if you skip sections that don't interest you, but I encourage you to go back to open your mind to other green topics. I encourage you to write in the margins, and get your family and friends involved. Be sure to visit www.stephaniebyng.com for more resources and updates to the book.

I strongly encourage you to join the Green Babes forum so you can be a part of the growing community. There you can discuss your experiences, post recipes; share your progress, and much more with fellow babes. You can even use the forum to network, make friends, and maybe join with other babes to start a green social group in your neighborhood. It's a great excuse to socialize, sample each other's favorite products, or even cook organic treats together. Visit www.stephaniebyng.com and click the Book Resources link to get to the forum.

I want this book to evolve with us, so I encourage you to write to me with your comments, critiques, product suggestions, and so on. You can reach me at babesguide@gmail.com.

How Green are you?

Take this quick yes/no quiz to see how green you are. To see how much you have improved, take this quiz now and after you have read the book. This allows you to quantify how green you are and keep track of areas for future improvement. If you want to find out what your carbon footprint is, try the calculator on **www.carboncounter.org**.

Beauty

- ❑ Do you know what the ingredients are in your cosmetics?
- ❑ Do you read the labels on your personal care products?
- ❑ Do you know what is in your nail polish?
- ❑ Do you use drug-store hair dye?
- ❑ Do you believe labels that say "natural" or "organic"?
- ❑ Do you use reusable menstrual products?
- ❑ Do you use certified organic personal care products?

Home

- ❑ Do you know what energy-efficient appliances are?
- ❑ Do you buy energy-efficient appliances?

- ❑ Do you know what compact fluorescent light bulbs (CFLs) or light emitting diodes (LED) are?
- ❑ Have you replaced at least one incandescent bulb in your house with a compact fluorescent light bulb (CFL) or LED?
- ❑ Do you purchase paper items made from recycled or post consumer material?
- ❑ Have you ever cleaned your refrigerator coils?
- ❑ Do you replace your AC/Heater filter every few months?
- ❑ Do you shut things off when not using them?
- ❑ Do you unplug appliances and chargers when not using them?
- ❑ Is your thermostat set at 68 degrees Fahrenheit or lower?

- Is your air conditioner set at 78 degrees Fahrenheit or higher?
- Is your water heater wrapped?
- Do you purchase green energy?
- Do you use your washer/dryer almost every day?
- Do you ever air dry your clothes?
- Do you take your clothes to a regular dry-cleaner?
- Do you have low flow toilets and showerheads?
- Do you have aerators on your faucets?
- Do you use recycled trash bags?
- Are you aware of how many bags of trash you generate weekly?
- Do you recycle?
- Do you use toxic cleaners in your home?
- Do you throw used batteries into the trash?
- Do you know what volatile organic compounds (VOCs) are?
- Are VOCs present in your home?
- Have you ever visited a hazardous waste facility?

- Do you have green houseplants in your home?
- Do all members of your family try to conserve water?

Yard

- Do you have a garden?
- Do you grow herbs?
- Do you know about native plants?
- Do you grow native plants?
- Do you use lawn fertilizer?
- Do you use garden pesticides?
- Is your garden organic?
- Do you irrigate your lawn every day?
- Do you hose your driveway to clean it off?

Car

- Do you drive an energy-efficient car?
- If not, are you considering purchasing one?
- Do you ever carpool?
- Do you drive to work every day?
- Do you own a bicycle?
- When you change your oil, do you recycle it?

- ❑ Do you check your tire pressure once a week?
- ❑ Do you change your air filter often?
- ❑ Do you wash your car at home?
- ❑ Do you avoid extra driving?

Shopping

- ❑ Do you buy organic cotton clothes or linens?
- ❑ Do you buy clothes not made with sweatshop labor?
- ❑ Do you know what Fair Trade is?
- ❑ Do you try to eat locally grown food?
- ❑ Do you eat organic food?
- ❑ Do you try to buy things with less packaging?
- ❑ Do you shop at farmer's markets?
- ❑ Do you buy from small local stores?
- ❑ Do you avoid factory-farmed meats?
- ❑ Do you buy organic produce?
- ❑ Do you buy hormone and antibiotic-free dairy and meats?

- ❑ Do you avoid frivolous or unnecessary shopping?
- ❑ Do you use reusable shopping bags?
- ❑ If you use plastic shopping bags, do you recycle them at the store?

Habits

- ❑ Do you use washable/reusable water bottles?
- ❑ Do you avoid purchasing bottled water?
- ❑ If you drink takeout coffee or tea, do you bring your own mug?
- ❑ Do you turn the water off when you brush your teeth, suds up your hair or shave?
- ❑ Do you read your magazines and newspapers online as opposed to getting a printed copy?
- ❑ Do you receive your bills electronically as opposed to in the mail/in print?
- ❑ When you print things at home, do you use both sides of the page?

Babes and their Bodies

The Moon-Wise Visitor

Girl, of all the places to start, why start here? Why not? Most women do it! Odds are you might be doing it right now. If you are wondering what I'm talking about, perhaps you recognize her by another name:

Aunt Flo, Big Red, Bleeding like a stuck pig, Blood of St. Menses, Carrie, Code red, Cousin Cramps, Crimson tide, Flooding, The Gift, Invasion of the Red Army, Leak week, The mean reds, Monsoon season, Moon-Time, On the Rag, Red Tent, Riding the Cotton Pony, Smoking a White Owl, The Flooding of the Topiary Garden, or Wrong time of the Month.

I think you get the point.

Greening your menstrual cycle is the quickest and easiest place to start. Conventional menstrual products such as Tampax, Kotex and Always have negative health and environmental impacts. These products dominate the feminine hygiene industry; in fact, you may be hard pressed to think of any menstrual product that is not a disposable pad or tampon. The first step to greening your period will be to switch to reusable products, which I will discuss in detail in a bit. First I would like to address the five main concerns with conventional disposable menstrual products.

1) Dioxin
2) Rayon
3) Environmental Devastation
4) High Cost
5) Negative Advertising

First, name brand manufacturers use a form of chlorine bleaching in order to whiten their product. The byproduct of this chemical bleaching process is a toxin called dioxin, which is linked to cancer, Toxic Shock Syndrome (TSS), and Endometriosis.[3] TSS occurs when poisons enter the bloodstream, in this case, through the vaginal walls. Symptoms can be high fever, rash, low blood pressure, and multiple organ failure[4]. Endometriosis is a medical condition where growths, tumors, implants, lesions, or nodules form near the uterus, bladder, and ovaries[5]. Even the Environmental Protection Agency is concerned about dioxin and believes that there is no acceptable level of exposure because the chemical is slow to disintegrate and accumulates over time. This means that every time you are exposed to it, it adds up in your body, reaching levels that may cause serious health problems. So the real danger comes from repeated contact to dioxin and if you use bleached pads or tampons regularly, you are exposing yourself to dioxin 4-5 times a day, five days a month, for 30-40 years.

The irony is that the whitening process is done only for marketing purposes. Manufactures thought the products would sell well if they were super white, because humans associate white with cleanliness. Beyond this, there are racial implications with the association between whiteness and cleanliness/goodness. This implies that anything not white is dirty, wrong, or unacceptable. I cannot emphasize this enough: **There is no medical reason for bleaching pads and tampons. It does not make them sterile[6].**

Second, there is a strong link between the ingredients of pads/tampons and the production of the bacteria causing TSS[7]. Over the years manufacturers have altered their products and the reported cases of TSS have gone down, but have not been eliminated. Most conventional tampons are made with a combination of cotton and rayon. Rayon is not vagina friendly. Rayon is highly absorbent and conventional tampons can leave bits of the material in the vagina. Tampons are so absorbent that they sap the vagina of its natural fluids. These fluids are essential to the health and wellbeing of your vagina. It's the equivalent of having a dry mouth where your tongue sticks and the skin in your mouth splits open/gets irritated. On top of this, rayon is coarse and can cause microscopic cuts. This is linked to vaginal ulceration (open sores) and peeling of the mucous membrane (vaginal walls), which creates a breeding ground for infection and sexually transmitted diseases[8].

On a quick side note, manufacturers are not required to label all of the ingredients, so you really don't know what else you are putting next to and into your vagina.

Third, conventional menstrual products contribute to environmental devastation because they are nonbiodegradable and disposable. Nonbiodegradable means that it will not decompose naturally like grass clippings or newspaper. It takes 500-800 years for pads and tampons to decompose[9]. This is an estimate that means that the product will not decompose during our lifetime. The average woman uses 16,800 sanitary pads and tampons in her lifetime and over 14 billion pads and tampons are put into North American landfills yearly[10]. The National Pollutant Release Inventory reports that, "pulp (used in tampons and pads) and paper is the third largest industrial polluter to air, water, and land both in Canada and the United States, and releases well over a hundred million kilograms of toxic pollution each year." In addition, 25% of all the insecticides in the United States are used on cotton. [11]

Fourth, conventional menstrual products are very expensive. One could potentially spend several thousand dollars during her menstrual lifetime on disposable products; whereas she could potentially spend a few hundred dollars on reusable products during her lifetime (See next section). One box of tampons/pads every month ($5-8 each) for 30-40 years equals $1800-3840. This cost does not included liners or other menstrual products that are often used[12].

Finally, conventional menstrual products are marketed and designed to hide the truth of menstruation[13]. Products are marketed to women to encourage them to hide the fact that they bleed by using materials that can be wrapped up and thrown away, thus adding to landfill waste. If you can't see it, it doesn't exist. To manufacturers, menstruation is a problem that needs to be solved, so they advertise discretion, modesty and cleanliness in their advertising. This often costs women their self-esteem and a positive menstrual experience[14].

A 2002 study on menstrual product advertising[15] found the following themes:

- In order to be confident, women need 'protection' from 'accidents.' This encourages women to 'maintain' their vaginas on a daily basis with liners, deodorants, PMS pills, and pads/tampons made in many shapes and sizes. Every day of the month is a day to hide the fact that you have a living vagina. Advertisers claim that all these products liberate women and offer them choice, but what it really does is enslave women to their vaginal maintenance and make women spend more money.

- To avoid embarrassment, women must not be caught menstruating. This is demonstrated in product packaging. Advertisers think that if they make packaging small and pink, then no one will know it's for collecting menstrual fluids.

- Women must appear "normal" (non-menstruating) at all times. Advertisements teach that the appearance of not having one's period is always the ideal feminine state. In other words, women must not be older than 10 years old. No wonder pedophilia exists, when society glorifies a child-like ideal for women.

- Women must not let their period prevent them from participating in normal and/or daily activities. This leaves women feeling ashamed for needed a moment to themselves during their period.

- Women stink and need to hide that stink at all times; hence women are dirty and unclean (being female = being dirty). The implication is that in the absence of these feminine hygiene products, a woman will not be able to achieve the ideal state of being fresh or clean due to her menstruating body.

- Tampon applicators exist, so women do not have to touch themselves. Again, this tells us that the vagina is so dirty, even women won't touch it.

21

Reusable Products[16]

All this is a lot to take in and may seem very daunting. But don't fret!
There are options and alternatives galore! The following products are
biodegradable, reusable, or organic, and have virtually no risk to the
user or the environment. There is a list of manufacturers and places to
buy at the end of this chapter.

Reusable Pads

Reusable pads are often made with 100%
cotton (organic and regular), hemp, wool
and bamboo. They can be handmade or
bought from retailers such as Lunapads,
Glad Rags, or Moon Pads. Retailers make
them in pretty prints and colors. They are
softer and more breathable than

disposable products, which contain glue and plastics. This also means
there is less irritation and no chance of getting glue stuck to your pubic
hair! Most manufacturers use clasps and/or buttons, so you get the same
reliability as the conventional products with wings. Reusable pads can
be hand washed or laundered. They do not stain the other items in the
wash. This product's reusability will save women hundreds to thousands
of dollars over their menstrual lifetime. In addition, there is nothing to
throw away, so there is no waste. They cost between $4 and $20 each,
depending on size. Liners cost around $2-5.

Ok, these sound perfect, there has to be a down side! Well that depends
on what you consider a down side. First, you have to be willing to wash
them. This means that you have to touch them! If you are grossed out,
you shouldn't be. It's just your menstrual fluid; something that your
body created. It's not like washing your brother's, husband's, or father's
streaked underwear! What I personally do is rinse them out as soon as I
can or when I get home. I then toss them in my laundry basket and just
wash them with clothes. No muss, no fuss. Some women keep a pretty
jar next to the toilet in which they put a few inches of water and a bit of

soap. They soak their pads in the jar until they are ready to wash them. If you hand wash your pads, they can get hard and crunchy, so a washing machine is recommended.

Second, they are not so convenient when you are out. You may have to carry the used pads home in a plastic bag. If you order your pads, most manufactures sell really cute vinyl carrying bags. Third, they can be bulky. I made mine, and because I have a light flow, mine are no thicker than conventional ultra-thin pads. Most manufacturers sell pads that have optional inserts, so you can make the pad as thin or thick as you need.

Finally, if you are active and you're wearing the wrong type of panties, they can move on you. The other day, I was playing basketball with some friends. I was wearing cheeky lace underwear from Lane Bryant and a panty liner. Not 15 minutes into the game and my pad had been pushed all the way to the back of my butt near my waste. This problem can be avoided by wearing snug fitting brief, hipster, or bikini cut underwear that is made from cotton or a cotton-like material. I now have special underwear set aside for when I'm menstruating, which means I don't mess up my pretty ones.

The Diva Cup

For those of you who like tampons, the Diva Cup or Keeper will become your new best friend. The Diva Cup is a cup made from medical grade silicone that is inserted into the vagina to collect menstrual fluids (The Keeper is made from latex). The cup is flexible and you fold it to insert it. Because it collects menstrual fluid, rather than absorbing it the way tampons do, there is no risk of contracting Toxic Shock  Syndrome. It doesn't strip you of your natural fluids, which are necessary for a healthy vagina, and it doesn't cut you like rayon. It sits near the entrance of the vagina and the vaginal muscles hold it in place. Like a tampon, you can't really feel it, and it does take practice to get

23

used to. It needs to be changed 2-4 times a day and can be worn overnight. This is an investment of about $30-40 every 10 years (that's how long manufactures suggest you use them before recycling them). There are two sizes available. In addition, there is nothing to throw away, so there is no waste.

Are there downsides? Of course. It takes a few tries to learn how to insert it properly. I actually practiced while I was not menstruating to insure I was good to go when 'game day' came. If you have difficulty inserting it, try adding a bit of water-based lubricant. It can be messy to change it, especially in a public bathroom, so I try to time it so I only change it while I'm in the shower. By changing it, I mean the process of pulling it out, cleaning it and then reinserting it. Some women don't feel comfortable in a public restroom to walk out, clean it in the sink and then walk back to the stall. To those women I say, if you can't feel comfortable with your period in a room dedicated to women, their menstruation, urination, and bowel movements, then where can you? However, Diva makes a wash that is in a small squirt bottle, so you can rinse and repeat in the privacy of your bathroom stall.

In addition, there are a few issues with fit. It only comes in 2 sizes, so it might not fit you perfectly. However, the general

An Eco-Babe's Tip:

I love the Diva Cup! Before using the Diva Cup, I tried a disposable menstrual cup, Softcup, and I had problems with it leaking. For that reason, I was hesitant to try the Diva Cup, but a friend was so enthusiastic about hers, I decided to give it a try. Boy, am I glad I did. I have never had a problem with leaking, it is comfortable, and I can wear it for up to twelve hours without emptying it. It is so convenient to not have to worry about changing it every few hours or having to go to the store and buy more products. I have even used it after having a baby without any problems. It takes a little practice to perfect the "twist" that creates the seal, but once you get it, you will never go back to paper products again. - **Lisa Pratt, Law Student and Mom to 5 children aged 3 months - 9 years, Springfield, VA**

consensus is that these cups rock! Some find that cutting a bit off the tip/handle helps with fit. The other issue with fit is that the suction effect is initially disconcerting. When tampons are pulled from the body, you can feel them fight you a little bit and you have to use firm pressure. That fighting is due to the muscles squeezing, and the suction caused by a difference in pressure from the inside and outside of the vagina. Well reusable cups are similar. You need to bear down with your vaginal muscles to assist in pulling the cup from your body. As it releases, you feel a strong suction. It's weird, but not so bad that you can't get used to it and it doesn't hurt. You may even hear a soft squelch sound as it releases.

Sea Pearls

Another option to tampons is Sea Pearls. Sea Pearls are natural Sea Sponge tampons. They are a renewable, dioxin and rayon-free alternative to conventional tampons. They have not been linked with TSS because they do not contain rayon. However I do suggest you exercise some caution because they still absorb your natural fluids. They are very affordable. Sponges are plant-like creatures that grow on the ocean floor. Don't let that scare you. They can be cut to size and you can tie a string around it for easy removal. Just like tampons, you can't feel them, but you need to change them more often. They are not loufas, and are very soft. I think these are a great starter to working up to the Keeper or Diva Cup because they are much easier to insert and remove.

There are a few downsides. As they are an animal product, they are not appropriate for strict vegans. Sea Pearls can be messy to change, especially in a public bathroom. Like reusable pads, it's important to have a bag to put used ones in when you are not home. They have to be changed more frequently than The Keeper and Diva Cup, and if you bleed heavily you might want to wear a thin washable pad as well, just in case. You also have to be sure to clean them really well, in order to avoid putting contaminants in your body. Finally, (this is funny, but not cool) when they are full they can fly out if you sneeze or laugh hard.

Organic Pads and Tampons

The final option is organic pads and tampons. They are very similar to conventional pads and tampons, except they are made of 100% organic cotton and are not bleached. They are still disposable and are more expensive than conventional products. Because they are not bleached, there is no dioxin, but there is still a risk of Toxic Shock Syndrome with the tampons. And of course, they still pollute the environment. I do not recommend this route because the cons outweigh the benefits. If you really want to do something better for the environment and you, one of the previous products or a combination thereof, should suffice.

An Eco-Babe Business Spotlight: Lunapads

Lunapads International is a women-owned small business based in Vancouver, Canada. Our mission is to help women have healthier and more positive experiences of their menstrual cycles, and by extension, their bodies overall. Our team is made up of a passionate group of gals who believe that using natural menstrual products is a creative and empowering way to honor and care for ourselves and the planet.

Lunapads offers a diverse selection of products designed to meet the unique needs of women of all ages. All our products have been created or chosen based on our own needs and lifestyles (in other words, we use them ourselves, and have done so for years), and we are confident we can find a solution that will work for you. We are completely committed to customer service and want to ensure that your experience with Lunapads is a positive one.

Since 1993, Lunapads has been making their signature collection of menstrual products, Lunapads and Lunapanties. Lunapads were created and designed by Madeleine Shaw, a fashion designer who realized she needed something to solve her own health concerns about using disposable pads and tampons. Switching from tampons to cloth pads brought her the unexpected benefit of discovering a deeper connection with her body, and she set out to bring this gift to other women in the form of starting a business. She wrote the first business plan for Lunapads in 1994, and in 1995 opened a store and small production facility. By 1998, Lunapads were available in health food stores across Canada.

In 1999 Madeleine met Suzanne Siemens, an accountant, at a Community Leadership course they were both participating in. Realizing that they shared a vision for better health for women and the planet, they combined their skills to fully develop Lunapads' potential. Lunapads are now used by thousands of women all over the world. Please visit **Lunapads.com** for more information[17].

Resources

Food and Drug Administration.
   (www.fda.gov/cdrh/consumer/tamponsabs.pdf)
Student Environmental Action Coalition. (www.seac)

Sewing Instructions to make your own
   Tiny Birds Organics
         (www.tinybirdsorganics.com/organiccotton/clothpads.
         html)
   Fuz Baby
         (www.fuzbaby.com/articles/makeyourown_clothmenst
         rualpads.htm)
   Many Moons Alternatives (www.manymoonsalternatives.com)
   WikiHow (www.wikihow.com/Make-Your-Own-Reusable-
         Menstrual-Pads)
   Jan Andrea (www.sleepingbaby.net/jan/Baby/PADS.html)
   Adahy's Cloth Pad Patterns
         (shewhorunsintheforest.googlepages.com)
   Women's Environmental Network (WEN)
         (www.wen.org.uk/sanpro/reports/makeyourown_web.
         pdf)

Beautification

The cosmetics industry is a $50 billion industry[18] worldwide. Some claim it to be recession proof! Have you every counted how many cosmetic/beauty products you use daily? What about your children? If you have a male spouse, he might even have his own beauty products, with that signature musk scent. Odds are it's over 10 and most people use these products without a second thought. We assume the government is regulating these products to ensure the safety of our families and ourselves. Sadly no. The government does not require testing or studies for personal care products[19]. The nonprofit organization, The Environmental Working Group (**www.ewg.org**) reports that people apply an average of 126 unique ingredients[20] on their skin daily. That's 126 ingredients that have not been tested for your safety or for the impacts they may have to animals and the environment.

First let's discuss personal care products and their effects on our bodies. In August 2005, scientists discovered that there is a relationship between phthalates, a chemical found in fragrances, and the feminization of male babies in the United States (meaning baby boys are born with female-like genitalia). Parabens, a common chemical preservative found in deodorant, has been found in breast tumor tissue. The Environmental Working Group (EWG) has been researching personal care product safety for over five years. Here is what they have found.[21]

Industrial chemicals, like those found in degreasers, carcinogens and pesticides are common ingredients in personal care products. In fact there are over 10,000 known industrial chemicals, such as coal tar and lead acetate, used as base ingredients in these products. The EWG compares the amount of toxins utilized to be like the 'flour' in a bread recipe. This means that they are used in fairly large quantities. These chemicals easily penetrate the skin and can also be ingested directly from our lips and hands.

28

These chemicals are approved for use often without testing for our safety. The FDA's Office of Cosmetics and Colors states that,**"...a cosmetic manufacturer may use almost any raw material as a cosmetic ingredient and market the product without an approval from FDA"**[22]. Almost 90% of the industrial chemicals used in personal care products have NEVER been tested by the FDA, CIR (Cosmetic Ingredient Review) or any other publicly accountable agency.

Are these products harming our health?

Like I mentioned before, our skin is the largest organ in our body and it is very absorbent. Our skin is not a one-way door, where sweat comes out, but nothing goes back in. Skin can absorb toxins not only through the skins cells, of which there are about 20 million, but also through hair follicles and sweat glands. Roughly 60 percent of what is applied to the skin can be absorbed directly into the blood stream. How can this be proven? Recently, there has been an influx of medications that are being administered through skin patches, such as nicotine and birth control. If you can absorb your birth control through your skin, doesn't it make sense that you could absorb your makeup and lotion too?

This is why rubbing lotion on our skin, actually softens it, and why our fingers become wrinkled when we bathe. Cosmetic ingredients are designed to penetrate the skin. This is the main selling point! How else is that crème supposed to remove wrinkles or tan your skin! One specialist, Dr. Haushka, estimated that a single woman could absorb about 30 pounds worth of moisturizer ingredients over the course of 60 years. Aveda, a company that chooses to use natural ingredients, estimates that during our lifetime, we eat four tubes of lipstick! I never thought about it that way before, but why else would companies make flavored lip balm? It's so we lick it off our lips and have to reapply more. Some of the more dangerous chemicals are penetration enhancers because they are put in place to make the product absorb into our skin.

Scientists have found many of these ingredients in human tissues such as phthalates in urine, parabens in breast tumor tissue, and musk xylene in human fat. The problem is that recent studies are showing that these ingredients are linked with health problems. More research needs to be done, but do you really want to take a chance that you are poisoning yourself and your family?

To learn about the safety of ingredients in personal care products, the Environmental Working Group has compiled an electronic database of ingredient labels for 32,065 name-brand products and cross-linked it with 49 toxicity or regulatory databases. You can view it at www.cosmeticsdatabase.com/special/whatnottobuy/

Are these products harming wildlife, and the environment?

Personal care products have negative effects on the hormone systems of wildlife, and the environment. Many millions of bottles, jars, tubes, and tissues of beauty products go into landfills and down the drain every year. There has been recent media attention on the quality of our drinking water. Recent studies have found hormones and anti-depressants, among other drugs, in our tap water. One way they get there is through our urine and bath water. Because the ingredients of personal care products are absorbed through our skin, they exit our system through urine, sweat, saliva, etc. In addition, every time we bathe; lotion, makeup, soap, and sweat get washed down the drain. We are flushing and washing our way to a polluted water supply.

Scientists have found personal care product ingredients in rivers and streams around the world, and some ingredients target the hormone system and are linked with the feminization of fish. Why feminization? It's because a large portion of chemicals in personal care products act like estrogen. It's as if we are giving estrogen supplements to our wildlife.

Take note of the chemicals used in your favorite products and research them. Odds are you will find that you are exposing yourself to a possible poison. Don't worry; I'm not going to leave you hanging there with a bathroom full of carcinogens and no options. The next section is all about shopping smart.

To get you started, here is the Environmental Working Group's list of the top 10 brands of concern. The brands listed below contain ingredients with the average highest levels of concern according to the rating system, from among the 179 brands with at least 40 products in Skin Deep's database. The average score is on a scale of 1 to 10, with 1 being no concern and 10 being high concern for safety. (For details please see **http://www.cosmeticsdatabase.com/about.php.**)

Rank	Brand	Company	# of Products in the Database	Average Score
1	Superior Preference	L'Oréal	40 products	9.0
2	Dark & Lovely	L'Oréal	66 products	7.4
3	Clairol	Procter & Gamble	466 products	6.9
4	Biotherm	L'Oréal	69 products	6.8
5	Clarins	Clarins of Paris	51 products	6.6
6	Revlon	Revlon Consumer Products Corp	443 products	6.4
7	Banana Boat	Playtex Products	89 products	6.4
8	Ultima II	Revlon Consumer Products Corp	47 products	6.3
9	No-Ad	Solar Cosmetic Labs, Inc.	46 products	6.3
10	Lancome	L'Oréal	57 products	6.3

For a list of alternative products, please visit
www.safecosmetics.org/companies/signers.cfm.
Safe, in this case, does not mean organic. It just means the company has signed a contract to make products that are free of chemicals that are known or strongly suspected of causing cancer, mutation or birth defects. For information about shopping organically, keep reading!

Shopping Organically

Now that you know about the dangers of chemicals in personal care products, it's time to review the world of organics. Shopping organically is not as easy as one would suspect, because manufacturers twist the truth. It's sad but true; they just want your money. Organic products are biodegradable and do not harm you or the environment, but there are several different levels of "organic-ness" that often confuse consumers.

Organic means free from all synthetic chemicals, including pesticides, herbicides, preservatives, artificial fragrances/colors/flavors, hormones, antibiotics, and anything man-made. In other words, organic means it was farmed using nothing but soil, sunshine and water. However, since interest in green living has exploded, some companies have taken the opportunity to scam us. The have flooded the markets with products labeled "healthy," "hypoallergenic," "unscented," "natural," "with certified organic ingredients" or even "with 100% certified organic ingredients," but really, they are full of synthetic materials. These labels lead you to believe that what you are buying is truly all-organic, but it could be that one single ingredient is 100% organic, and the rest are all synthetic. Therefore, the label is misleading but true. Others will say things like "no phosphates" to give the impression that they are chemical free. Once again, the impression is that it is natural, but in reality, it just doesn't contain that particular chemical.

Another sneaky tactic is to claim being "environmentally-friendly" even though the product is in a nonbiodegradable container. This means you have to be an informed and merciless consumer. Don't worry; I will give you tips to make organic shopping a breeze.

There are several other tricks that manufactures use to get your money.[23] Some will outright lie and the FDA doesn't have the time or resources to do anything about it! It is illegal, but manufactures have to be caught. If you are unsure of any product, skip it.

One trick is to use water. Most cleansing and beauty products have a lot of water in them. In fact, it is most often the first ingredient in the product. To make a product appear natural, they will turn the water into a weak tea infusion of some trendy and exotic herbs like green tea and acai berry. Because they are in the water, they will be listed first on the label, even if they are barely there. Most consumers will focus on the fancy plant names and images of leaves and ignore the rest of the label. I know I have been suckered into this one.

Here's another water trick. Water is not an agricultural product (meaning it's not grown), so it can't be organic. When calculating the percentage of organic ingredients, the USDA says you are not allowed to count the water portion of a product, because if you could count it, it would be deceptive. Some companies choose to ignore this regulation. Imagine if you made a weak tea using all organic herbs and added that to a blend of synthetic materials. If water was 70% of the product, you could say the product was 72% organic rather than the 2% organic from the few organic herbs you used in the water. There is a big difference between 72% and 2% organic.

Would you ever call gasoline "natural"? Why not? It's "derived from" plants and dinosaurs! Believe it or not, some companies will use this play on words to pass off oils and chemicals as natural. The two kinds of synthetic chemicals, petrochemicals (made from crude petroleum) and oleochemicals (made from plant oils) can be processed in factories and turned into just about anything by using pressure, high temperatures, and other chemicals. They are by definition and according to the USDA, synthetic. However, manufacturers will say that they are "derived from" natural sources. One way they show this is by putting the name of the chemical, next to the name, in parenthesis, of the natural product it was derived from. Here is an example from a shampoo I used to adore: "amyl acetate (banana fragrance)". Are there really bananas in my old shampoo? No, but it contains oleochemicals that were cooked and morphed to look like those extracts. They must think we are idiots!

So now that you know the dangers of beauty products and how to spot real organic products, it's time to go shopping. The first thing you need to do is learn how to read labels. Just because a product is sold at a natural foods store, doesn't mean it's organic and safe. However, odds are that most products in mainstream food, drug, and department stores are not organic, so if you're shopping at a natural foods store, you have greatly increased your chances of finding a great organic product. Here are some quick tips to remember:

Not tested on animals – While the finished product may not have been tested on animals, this doesn't mean that the individual ingredients weren't tested on animals. So make sure you look for other organic clues before you purchase. Keep Shopping.

Natural, hypoallergenic – These terms mean absolutely nothing. Keep shopping.

Organic –Keep a look out for the "USDA Organic" seal, a statement of certification from the California Organic Farmers Association (COFA), or "100% Organic" from a reliable state or local body. In order to be certified organic, a product must contain at least 95% organic ingredients, not counting the water.

There are three levels of organic certification by the USDA.

100% Organic – This means that product is all organic.

Organic – This means that the product contains 95% organic ingredients.

Made with Organic Ingredients – This means that the product contains at least 70% organic ingredients.

The green and white USDA logo will only be used on 100% organic and organic products. If you are unsure about a product, move on. If you don't see a USDA organic logo or some other certification guarantee, don't buy it. Keep shopping.

Avoid certain unpronounceable ingredients– Keep an eye out for products in which ALL of the ingredients have names that you could find in a seed catalog or nontoxic minerals like clay. Here is a partial list of some ingredients to avoid, based on information from **www.beautytruth.net**. Every side effect and health hazard can be found on the Material Safety Data Sheets (MSDS) that manufacturers are required by law to make. You can see a break down of these at **http://www.care2.com/c2c/share/detail/664208**. **You will find this list reprinted in the appendices, so you can rip it out and take it with you to the store.**

- ✓ Methyl, Propyl, Butyl and Ethyl Parabens – These are petroleum based preservatives. They can be found in almost all non-organic hair and skin products. These preservatives act like estrogen, and can cause cancer, hormone imbalances, and low sperm count.

- ✓ Coal Tar – This is found in most dandruff shampoos and anti-itch creams. It is a known carcinogen. When used as dye, it can be found in toothpaste (FD&C Blue 1) and mouthwash (FD&C Green 3).

- ✓ Sodium Lauryl Sulfate and Sodium Laureth Sulfate (SLS) – These ingredients add foam/sudsing/frothing power to personal care products. They are related to bladder/kidney/urinary tract infections, rash, eye irritation, HAIR LOSS (yes they use it in almost ALL shampoos!), and dandruff. So-called "natural" products use these ingredients and cover it up by saying it's derived from coconut.

- ✓ Hydroquinone – This is found in facial lotions and skin lighteners. It is a known neurotoxin.

- ✓ Formaldehydes also known as: DMDM hydantoin, Quaternium 15, Diazolidinyl Urea, Imidazolidinyl Urea, 2-bromo-2-nitropropane-1, 3-diol – These products are also preservatives and are liked with inability to urinate, rashes, irritated mucus membranes, and internal bleeding. These are known carcinogens.

✓ <u>Synthetic Colors labeled as FD&C or D&C, followed by a color and a number</u> – These are made from coal tar, lead, and aluminum salts and can cause lead toxicity. This is especially dangers to children, the elderly and pregnant women. They are also linked with cancer, asthma, eczema, hyperactivity, headaches, itchy and watery eyes, and blurred vision.

✓ <u>Synthetic Fragrances often labeled simply as "fragrance"</u>- There are about 200 ingredients that this could refer to, most of which are toxic, and neurotoxins (neurotoxin means it can damage or destroy nerve tissue including tissues in the brain). They can cause headaches, dizziness, rashes, skin discoloration, coughing fits, vomiting, behavioral changes (depression, hyperactivity), and hormonal changes (mimics estrogen). They are stored in body fat and have been found in breast milk.

✓ <u>Parraffin</u> (mineral oil, petroleum) – Another petroleum based ingredient that is a wax, mineral oil or petrolatum jelly. This ingredient makes you sensitive to the sun, interferes with the skin's natural moisturizing mechanism, and also acts like estrogen. It's ironically found in chap sticks, lip balm, lip stick, and lotions among other personal care products.

✓ <u>Triclosan</u> – This is found in most antibacterial products, as well as toothpaste and makeup. It is often found with dioxin which can decrease fertility, weaken the immune system and cause birth defects.

✓ <u>Alcohol, isopropyl (SD-40)</u> – A petroleum based ingredient. This can be found in many products from hair spray and perfume, to antibacterial hand wash and antifreeze. It strips your skin of moisture and makes you vulnerable to bacteria, mold, fungus and viruses. This is ironic considering it's found in many antibacterial products. It's also known to cause brown spots and premature aging of the skin as well as headaches, dizziness, depression, nausea and vomiting. One ounce is considered a FATAL dose.

✓ Aluminum – Aluminum can affect how the body uses certain minerals like calcium, phosphorus and iron. It's related to neurological disorders such as Alzheimer's, Parkinson's, and dementia. It is a known carcinogen and mutagenic, and is used as a coloring agent. You will find it in most personal care products, like eye shadow, hair dye, and antiperspirants.

✓ Lead and Mercury (lead acetate and thimerosol) – These are more well known neurotoxins, because of all the media coverage concerning fish. It is found in toothpaste and men's hair dye.

✓ Mainstream Sunscreen with the following ingredients: Octyl-Dimethyl-Para-Amino-Benzoic Acid and Oxybenzone – These are ironically linked with skin cancer. A better alternative is a sunscreen with Titanium Dioxide in it. It's a natural mineral.

✓ p-Phenylenediamine (1,4-Benzenediamine, p-Phenyldiamine, 4-Phenylenediamine)– This is found in most do-it-yourself hair dyes. It is linked with damage to the nervous system, damage to the lungs, and severe allergic reactions.

Others to watch out for: Polyethylene Glycol (PEG), Talc, Acrylates, Methacrylates, Tocopherol Acetate, anything with the word 'paraben' in it,benzalkonium chloride, cetrimonium bromide, quaternium-15, quaternium 1-29, anything with the world 'chloride' in it, benzyl alcohol, carbomers, dimethicone, dimethicone copolyol, cyclomethicone.

An example of a great organic brand is Dr. Bronner's brand. I'm currently using Dr. Bronner's Magic Organic Fair Trade Shikakai Soap in Spearmint-Peppermint scent as my body soap. Right on the front of the bottle is the USDA Organic logo as well as the Fair for Life Fair

Trade logo (read more about fair trade in the "What are you wearing" chapter). On the ingredients side of the bottle, all of the ingredients are listed and I can recognize every one. There is not a single "polybutylwhatever" in the ingredients. Those that are fair trade are marked with an asterisk and denoted as "certified fair trade by IMO" (Institute for Marketecology).

Even further, the product is also certified organic by Oregon Tilth (OTCO) and certified no animal testing by the Coalition for Consumer information on Cosmetics (CCIC rabbit and stars logo). In addition, the bottle itself is made with 100% post-consumer recycled plastic. If I needed anymore clarification, there is also an explanation into how the product was made, why the ingredients are great and what the company's values are. This is the type of product you should be looking for and coincidentally, Target has just started carrying it in their stores!

Try not to be weirded out by the writing on the original castile soap bottle. It has to do with the outdated philosophy of Dr. Bronner, who is now deceased. The Dr. Bronner's website states that: "The over 30,000 words spread across all the soap labels were Dr. Bronner's life work of searching every religion and philosophy for "Full Truths.'" He was an eccentric but made great soap, so overlook the weirdness and enjoy![24]

I must take a moment to discuss Burt's Bees. Whenever I talk about organic products, people often say, "oh, like Burt's Bees?" Sadly, no. Burt's Bees does not sell any organic products. In fact, many of their new products contain synthetic fragrances. Even their new supposed organic bar soaps contain "fragrance." Remember 100% natural does not mean 100% organic. They are not certified organic by any authority. They are owned by Clorox. In my opinion, Burt's Bees is just a big company, out to make profit by confusing consumers and using misleading advertising. For a great article about the reality of Burt's Bees, please visit:
http://theorganicbeautyexpert.typepad.com/the_organic_beauty_expert/2008/02/mike-burt-and-t.html

and: http://www.dld123.com/q&a/index.php?cid=4124

Before you go shopping, look at your current personal care products to see what the ingredients are. If you are like me and on a budget, you can't afford to run out and replace everything you use. So count how many of the bad ingredients are in each product and make two piles. The first pile will be things that have a large amount of bad ingredients and should be thrown away and replaced immediately. The second pile is for things that have several bad ingredients, but you figure you can use up the product before you find a suitable replacement. If you have any questions concerning any of the ingredients, be sure to check out the Environmental Working Group's website at www.ewg.org, Safe Cosmetics www.safecosmetics.org, and Skin Deep at www.cosmeticsdatabase.com.

If you can't find organic products in your grocery store, you can request them by talking to or writing to the manager. If that doesn't work, try purchasing online, or find the next best thing in a natural, unscented, dye-free, chemical-free product preferably in recycled packaging.

**Be sure to read the next section as it has very important information about what your hair will do when you transition to organic products.

No 'Poo

Have you heard of this? No it's not about THAT! It's about living without shampoo. Believe it or not, it is possible. All you need is some baking soda, apple cider vinegar, and a few weeks without any major social engagements. Transitioning to a no 'poo lifestyle has a downside, and that is your hair may get a bit weird for a few weeks while your hair detoxes and you figure out the amounts of baking soda and apple cider vinegar you need. But once you get through that, you will love your hair. No 'poo should work for all hair types.

I know what you're thinking. You think your hair will turn into a big oily mess without your arsenal of styling products. Surprisingly that is not the case. The best metaphor I ever read compared your hair and scalp oils to breast feeding. The more your baby wants milk, the more your body produces it. If you suddenly stopped letting your baby nurse, your breasts would get engorged with milk. So for some time after you stop nursing your breasts will feel like they are over producing milk. After your body figures out that you are no longer nursing, your breasts will stop making milk. Your body returns to a state of balance.

Your hair works the same way. The demands we put on our hair and the products we use, strip away our natural oils. This triggers our scalp to make more oil to compensate. If you suddenly stop using those products, then your body will still overproduce oils. After a bit of time, your scalp will return to normal. So when you initially switch to no 'poo or even organic soaps, you hair and body will go through a period of adjustment where things may seem a bit greasier or dryer than normal. Trust me, it's all worth it. The transition period can be 2 weeks to 2 months depending on the person and how much detoxing needs to be done. Use that time to experiment and adjust what you use and how much. Some products that are only partially organic and contain a few bad ingredients will work just like normal shampoo with no transition period. For example, I used to use Aveda shampoo, which has a moderate hazard rating from Skin Deep (www.cosmeticsdatabase.com) and it worked just like conventional shampoos with a high hazard rating. The lower the hazard rating, the higher the chance of a weird transition period. But like I said, it's all worth it.

Here's how it works:
Measurements may be different for everyone. So start with 1 tablespoon of baking soda and use more or less depending on need.

- Dissolve about 1 tablespoon of baking soda in just enough water to make a paste. Apply this to your roots only. Work the paste in, and let it sit for about a minute. This is a good time to give yourself a scalp massage. It stimulates blood flow and cleans your pores. Picture a crown on your head. Start with the back of the crown, work your way to your hair part and fill in the circle. Do the back of your skull and temple region last. Scrub in small circles with your fingertips. Be gentle as you don't want to break your hair.
- Rinse the baking soda out of your hair.
- Mix 2 tablespoons of apple cider vinegar with a cup of water. Pour this mixture over the ends of your hair. Let it sit for a minute and then rinse it out.

If you hair becomes frizzy from the previous instructions, use less baking soda and/or leave it on for a shorter amount of time. Some people find it helpful to add a bit of honey to the baking soda mixture.

If your hair becomes greasy, try using less apple cider vinegar and make sure you are only applying it to the ends of your hair. You could also try rinsing with lemon or lime juice instead. I find it helpful to use a comb instead of a brush to brush out my hair.

If your hair is dry, apply a bit of oil to the underside of your hair. I prefer olive oil, but any will work.

If your scalp itches, add a few drops of essential oil to the baking soda mixture. I like lavender, rosemary, peppermint, and tea tree.

My Personal Beauty Regime

After all this, you may be wondering what I personally use. Remember, everyone is different, so you may need to experiment to find the organic products that are right for you.

- **Shampoo** – Avalon Organics Everyday Shampoo
- **Body Soap** – Dr. Bronner's Organic Shikakai Spearmint Peppermint Body Soap
- **Deodorant** – Bubble and Bee's Lemongrass Rosemary 100% Organic Deodorant
- **Lotion** – Dr. Bronner's Orange Lavender Organic Lotion (smells awesome)
- **Chapstick** – Burt's Bees Beeswax Lip Balm
- **Skin Balm** – Dr. Bronner's Patchouli Lime Organic Body/Tattoo Balm
- **Toothpaste** – Still shopping and using up Crest
- **Hand Soap** – Still shopping and using up Bath & Body works

In writing this book, I have discovered many great brands and products and I can't wait to try them all. As I run out of each product, I will try something new and post reviews on my website at **www.stephaniebyng.com.**

Resources

About Burt's Bees:
http://theorganicbeautyexpert.typepad.com/the_organic_beauty_expert/2008/02/mike-burt-and-t.html
http://www.dld123.com/q&a/index.php?cid=4124
About safe beauty products:
Environmental Working Group's (www.ewg)
Safe Cosmetics (www.safecosmetics.org)
Beauty Truth (www.beautytruth.net)
Skin Deep (www.cosmeticsdatabase.com/about.php.)

Recipes for Beauty

Ok, so you've read all this and your thinking "Why don't I make my own body care products?" Well why not! Some beauty products can be made at home, others…not so well. For those of you ready to go into the foray of homemade, here are some recipes. And for those of you who are ready to shop, there are resources for buying organic makeup, nail, and hair care products at the end.

Bar Soap

The first thing you want to do is invest in the right soap-making supplies as they can have a considerable effect on your finished product and vary depending on your method. Supplies do not have to be expensive, in fact some can already be found in your kitchen! Just remember that durable equipment will save you time, money and possible injury.

If you're feeling a little unsure of yourself, you might want to consider soap making kits. They come in a wide variety and can be found in local craft stores, novelty soap shops and online. Each kit contains a recipe, pre-measured ingredients and sometimes, additives, colorants and molds. Kits also vary in output, so you can start small with a few bars, or go big with enough to give out as presents! The price of the kits depends on how much they make but average around $10 to $30 per pound of soap, which is actually cheaper than the organic soap you can buy in stores.

There are four types of soap-making kits. The first is a Hot Process kit where you melt the ingredients and pour them into a mold. These are the easiest to do and come in glycerin, goat's milk, and seasonal kits. They usually contain a soap base, some fragrance and a recipe sheet. Make sure the ingredients are organic, as there are many chemical based kits on the market. Fragrances should be essential oils. Most craft stores sell these items individually if you would prefer a different color/scent/mold. The second is a Cold Process kit, which usually contains pre-measured oils, lye, essential oil/fragrance, a thermometer, and a recipe sheet. The third are Specialized Soap kits, which are for making baby soap, fizzy soap, shaving soap, moisturizing soap, acne soap, and aromatherapy soap. These may be harder to find at local craft stores. The final type of kit is the Refill kit. When you use up the ingredients from the previous 3 kits, you can purchase the refill kit and just follow the directions from the original. This way, if you find one you love, you can purchase the refill kit, usually at a cheaper rate.

If you want to dive in and skip the kits, here are the supplies you need.
- Soap Base – This makes the job of making soap very easy. It is used in the Hot Process and can be found in many varieties including glycerin, Castile, and goat milk. You melt it and then add fragrances, colors and oils to enhance them.
- Lye – This is used in the Cold Process. It's used to make the Cold Process soap base by adding water and fats/lard. *(Safety Note) When working with lye, it is best to follow safe practices and wear protective equipment. Safety glasses, a facemask, gloves and long sleeves are a must to protect you from accidental splashes and the fumes from the lye. Work in a well-ventilated area.*
- Fixed or Carrier Oil – (like sweet almond oil) These are added to enrich the soap so you can beautify your skin while you clean it.
- Essential Oils for Fragrance – These give the soap its scent. Essential oils (EO) can be expensive, but I prefer them to chemical fragrances, which can irritate skin. EOs can improve your skin while at the same time be used for aromatherapy. EOs are the kick that turn regular soap into gourmet soap. *(Safety Note) Essential oils are volatile and are highly flammable. Avoid contact with eyes. Use Safety gear.*
- Natural Ingredients and Additives – (like finely ground apricot seeds) These give your soap unique qualities like exfoliating, moisturizing, anti-acne, etc.
- Molds – Soap molds come in a wide variety of forms that range from novelty holiday shapes, to flowers and circles.

- Colorants – These of course add color to the soap. Experiment and try to play with color/shape/scent for an attractive package. Some people use food coloring.
- Utensils - You need a stainless steel or enamel pot, double-boiler, mixing bowl, a weighing scale, plastic or stainless steel spoon, apron, goggles, rubber gloves, thermometer, pitcher, and a blender or mixer. Keep the tools you use for soap making separate from those for food preparation.

How to Make Basic Glycerin Soap

Here is a step-by-step guide to making melt-and-pour glycerin soap:

1. Prepare a pound of glycerin soap base on a double-boiler or in a microwaveable container. It's easier to control the temperature when you heat it on a stove. Bring water to a boil, turn heat on low, add the base, and stir occasionally. Do not leave unattended. If you choose the microwave, make sure you cover the bowl with Saran Wrap to keep the excess moisture from evaporating out. Heat the base to around 55C or 155F then remove from the heat.

2. Add coloring to the melted base and mix well. Be wary of bubbles forming. If you see bubbles, allow them to get to the top and then spray them with rubbing alcohol to make them disappear. To use food coloring, simply put in 1 drop at a time to your melted base and color to preference. Too much can stain hands and towels, so be careful!

3. Add in fragrance and other desired additives and mix thoroughly. Start with .25 ounce of fragrance or EO per pound of base and work up or down from there.

4. Once everything is mixed well and no bubbles are formed, pour the mixture into your soap mold.

6. Set the soap aside for thirty minutes to sixty minutes then put in

the freezer for another thirty minutes.

7. Remove it from the freezer. Allow it to sit for a few minutes, and then unmold.

8. Tightly wrap finished soap with plastic to prevent attracting moisture.

The key to proper glycerin soap is to keep the heat as low as possible. It can get murky or have a beaded appearance if you heat it too high, too fast.

Cold Process Soap

There are serious safety issues associated with lye, which are beyond the scope of this book. For that reason I suggest you find a book specifically about making cold process soap. A good book to start with is Susan Cavitch's The SoapMakers Companion. When handling lye, please use gloves, goggles and a facemask, and work in a well-ventilated area.

Gourmet Beauty Recipes

For The Face

The following companies have generously allowed their beauty recipes to appear in this book. For more recipes and information, please visit their websites.

SpaIndex.com: Guide to Day Spas and Stay Spas www.spaindex.com
Spa Index Media, LLC 1511 M Sycamore, Suite 104 Hercules, CA 94547. 877-832-6169 - Toll Free Message Center

The National Honey Board www.honey.com
Note: Honey should not be fed to infants under one year of age. Honey is a safe and wholesome food for children and adults. © National Honey Board 11409 Business Park Circle Ste 210, Firestone, CO 80504 Phone: (303) 776-2337 Fax: (303) 776-1177

Almond Facial Milk (Spa Index)

The herbal waters are antiseptic and toning. Grapefruit seed extract is available in health food stores, and is included in the recipe as a preservative.

½-cup rose, lavender, or distilled water
1-teaspoon pure vegetable glycerin
1/4 to 1-teaspoon cold pressed organic almond oil
12-drops grapefruit seed extract

Make the rose or lavender water by placing a small handful of dried organic rose petals or lavender in a pint mason jar and adding boiling water to cover. Let steep overnight, then thoroughly strain. Combine the remaining ingredients in a glass jar and shake to blend. Dab some on your fingers or a cotton ball and massage into your skin. Rinse with warm water. Keep stored in the refrigerator for no more than a month or so. Discard at the first sign of mold.

Aloha Honey Hawaiian Delight (Honey Board)

- Makes 2 treatments -

½-ripe papaya
½-cup fresh pineapple, diced
2-Tbsp. green tea
2-Tbsp. honey

Steep green tea in boiling water. Set aside to cool. Peel papaya wedge and remove seeds. In blender or food processor, blend papaya and pineapple until pureed. Pour into glass bowl and combine honey and green tea. Mix well. Apply to face with fan brush or fingertips. Recline and rest for 10 – 15 minutes. Remove completely with tepid water and soft facial cloth. Store in covered container in refrigerator for up to one week.

Apple Cucumber Facial Mask (Spa Index)

½-cucumber, peeled
1-egg white
½-teaspoon lemon juice
½-teaspoon lime juice
½-teaspoon apple mint leaves
1-drop lime essential oil

Combine all 5 ingredients in a food processor and process until smooth. Add the essential oil last and mix well. Refrigerate the mixture for 10 minutes. Apply a layer to your clean face and neck area and leave it on for 20 minutes. Rinse well with warm water. Apple Cucumber Facial Mask is best when used immediately as the ingredients are perishable. The leftovers can be refrigerated in the coldest section of the refrigerator for up to 1-2 days but should be discarded after that.

Avocado Carrot Cream Mask (Spa Index)

This mask combines avocados, which are rich in Vitamin E, with carrots, which are high in beta-carotene and antioxidants, and cream, which is high in calcium and protein. These ingredients will rebuild skin collagen, improve tone and texture, and fade age spots.

1-avocado, mashed
1-carrot, cooked and mashed
½-cup heavy cream
1-egg, beaten
3-tablespoons honey

Combine all ingredients in a bowl until smooth. Spread gently over your face and neck, and leave in place 10-15 minutes. Rinse with cool water and follow with your favorite toner.

Basil Acne Tonic (Spa Index)

Basil is known for its "soothing and toning" properties.
2 to 3-teaspoons dried basil leaves
1-cup boiling water

Steep basil leaves in water for 10 to 20 minutes. Cool, and then apply to face with a white cotton ball. Keep tonic refrigerated. Recommended shelf life: 90 days.

Blueberry Toner (Spa Index)

Make this mask the day you plan to use it, and <u>do not store.</u>

3-tablespoons steamed, crushed blueberries
½-cup sour cream or plain yogurt

Purée ingredients in a blender at low speed until well mixed and fluffy. Apply to face and neck. Let penetrate for 15-20 minutes. Rinse off with tepid water. If you find the mask is too runny after blending, you should refrigerate for one hour or until of the consistency you desire.

Chocolate Facial Mask (Spa Index)

This decadent mask is actually an excellent moisturizer -- it leaves your skin baby soft. Recommended for normal skin.

1/3-cup cocoa powder
3-tbsp. heavy cream
2-tsp. cottage cheese
¼-cup honey
3-tsp. oatmeal

Mix all ingredients together (a bullet blender is ideal) and smooth onto face. Relax for ten 10 minutes, then wash off with warm water.

Firming Face Mask (Honey Board)

1-Tablespoon honey
1-egg white
1-teaspoon glycerin (available at drug and beauty stores)
Approx. 1/4-cup flour

Whisk together all ingredients and enough flour to form a paste (approximately 1/4 cup). Smooth over face and throat. Leave on 10 minutes. Rinse off with warm water.

Harvest Pumpkin Exfoliating Mask (Honey Board)

Makes 4 treatments.

4-Tbsp. pumpkin puree
1-Tbsp. honey
4-tsp. cornmeal
2-tsp. Aloe Vera gel
2-tsp. pineapple, diced
1-tsp. green tea
½-tsp. sunflower oil
6-drops frankincense essential oil (optional)
4-drops cinnamon extract (optional)

Steep green tea in a cup boiling water. Set aside to cool. In blender or food processor puree pineapple and place in medium-sized mixing bowl. Add pumpkin, honey and aloe. Mix well. Stir in sunflower oil, 1-tsp of green tea and cornmeal. Drink the remaining green tea. Add frankincense and cinnamon. Stir. Apply small amount of pumpkin mask to cheeks, forehead, chin and neck. Massage in circular motions gently buffing skin. Repeat. Apply more product as needed. Leave a thin layer of pumpkin mask on face and neck for 15-20 minutes. Rinse with tepid or cool water and pat dry with soft towel. Follow with appropriate moisturizer. Store remaining mask covered in refrigerator for up to 2 weeks.

Strip it Off! Pore Cleaning Strips (Spa Index)

This recipe makes a pore cleaning "strip" which works just like those sold in popular drugstores.

1-Tbsp   Knox unflavored gelatin
1 and ½-Tbsp milk

Mix two ingredients and microwave for 10 seconds to slightly warm. Using a clean cosmetic brush, apply to nose and chin area. Avoid delicate eye area. Rinse brush immediately. Allow mixture on nose and chin to dry for 10-15 minutes. Mixture will dry quite stiff and form a "stiff film." Peel off the film and stare at all the little porcupine quills that used to be in your nose pores (one of the chief entertainment factors with B'Strips!)

Tomato Blemish Remedy (Spa Index)

1-tomato, ripe, chopped
1-tsp. lemon juice
1-Tbsp instant style oatmeal or old fashioned rolled oats

Blend all ingredients until just combined, in a paste. Apply to blemished skin, making sure the mixture is thick enough to stay in place. Leave in place 10 minutes. Remove with damp washcloth, and rinse and tone.

Yin and Yang Honey Whip (Honey Board)

- Makes 3-4 treatments -

2-Tbsp. cocoa butter
1-tsp. honey
½-tsp. grated beeswax
½-tsp. ginseng powder
½-tsp. soy powder

Zest of mandarin, optional

In small double boiler melt cocoa butter and beeswax; stir slowly until completely melted. Pour into microwave safe dish. Add honey and stir until mixture has blended completely. Add ginseng and soy powder. Stir until mixture is a creamy consistency. Add zest of mandarin. To use, apply small amount to cheeks, forehead, chin and neck. Gently spread product until entire face is covered. May be left on skin for deep hydration or removed after 30 minutes. To remove, splash face with tepid or cool water. Pat dry with soft towel. Store remaining whip in dry place away from sun exposure. It may be necessary to slightly melt contents before applying, as the cocoa butter and beeswax may solidify.

For The Body

Antiperspirant/Deodorant (Spa Index)

Antiperspirants work by clogging, closing, or blocking the pores with powerful astringents -- such as aluminum salts -- so that they cannot release perspiration. Many natural health care proponents argue against using aluminum because it accumulates in the brain. Deodorants work by neutralizing the smell of the perspiration mixed with "body dust" (skin, hair and other bacterial goodies we carry around on ourselves all day), and by antiseptic action against that bacterium. Deodorants are more healthful because they don't interfere with perspiration, a natural cooling process. Here are a few simple recipes, which are fun to make because they can be customized with your favorite scents.

An Eco-Babe Tip:
I started using witch hazel based deodorants at a wedding. One of my fellow bridesmaids swore by it. Since we had on sleeveless red satin gowns there was no room for a flaky, white underarm mess. I tried it and haven't gone back to regular deodorant-antiperspirants since. Witch hazel is easy enough to apply: You can dab it on with cotton or a washcloth, or splash it on. **– Nina Ricci, English Teacher, South Korea**

52

Deodorant

Basic Deodorant Powder: 1/2 cup baking soda, 1/2 cup corn
few drops essential oils such as lavender or cinnamon, or try c
sage for men. Place the ingredients in a glass jar. Shake to blend.
Sprinkle a light covering of the powder on a damp washcloth. Pat on.
Do not rinse.

Basic Liquid Deodorant: 1/4 cup each witch hazel extract, aloe vera
gel, and mineral water, 1 teaspoon vegetable glycerin, a few drops
antibacterial essential oils such as lavender, or tea tree. Combine the
ingredients in a spray bottle. Shake to blend. Makes 3/4 cup with an
indefinite shelf life.

Morning Buzz Body Scrub (Honey Board)

Benefits: Rids the skin of dry patches and aids in circulation. Helps to
reduce cellulite while it firms and tones. Leaves skin smooth and supple.
Makes 1-2 treatments.

¼-cup freshly ground coffee
¼-cup buttermilk
2-Tbsp. wheat germ
2-Tbsp. honey
1-Tbsp. grapeseed oil
1-egg white

In mixing bowl, combine buttermilk, honey, grapeseed oil and egg
white, mix thoroughly. Slowly add coffee and wheat germ being careful
not to clot or clump. Scrub should be smooth and creamy but with a
slight grit. Let stand. Apply all over in shower or bath using a washcloth
or body sponge to aid in exfoliation. Rinse completely. Towel dry and
apply moisturizer. Chill remaining scrub if necessary.

Dry Skin Crème (Spa Index)

1/2-cup water
1/2-cup sesame seed oil
2-teaspoons vitamin E oil
2-tablespoons grated beeswax
3-drops essential oil of grapefruit
2-drops of aroma oil (optional, your choice)
A pinch of borax

Blend the vitamin E oil, beeswax and sesame oil. Heat on low until melted. Combine the water, oils and borax. Heat for a few minutes (until warm) but do not boil. Combine the water mixture with the beeswax mixture. Mix well (at least 2 minutes). For a fluffier cream, use an electric mixer or a blender. Pour the cream into a clean container after it has cooled completely.

End of Summer Almond Body Scrub (Spa Index)

2/3-cup ground almonds
1/3-cup oatmeal
½-teaspoon of herbs (lavender, chamomile, etc) (optional)
Plain yogurt, milk, or buttermilk, sufficient to make a paste
Essential Oils for scent (optional)

Combine the dry ingredients in a blender or food processor until they are reduced to a coarse meal. Keep this "scrub base" in a glass jar with a screw top in your refrigerator until ready to use. When you want to use the scrub base, scoop out 1/4 cup into a small bowl, and stir in enough of the liquid ingredients (vary it by what you have on hand -- yogurt and milk are best, but water works) to make a paste. Yogurt and milk are natural exfoliates known as alpha hydroxy acids, and they will slough off dead skin cells even without the scrub. Scoop up the paste with your hands or a washcloth, and rub over your body to exfoliate peeling skin. Rinse thoroughly

Gentle Honey Cleanser (Honey Board)

This cleanser is simple and effective. The soap gently clea
glycerin prevents drying and the honey not only softens the sk..
antimicrobial properties can help ward off breakouts. A touch of hon..
is all you need for healthy, glowing skin.

¼-cup honey
1-Tablespoon liquid soap
½-cup glycerin (available at drug and beauty stores)

Mix all ingredients together in a small bowl until they are fully blended.
Pour into a clean plastic bottle. Pour onto clean face sponge or soft cloth
and gently rub onto face, wash away with warm water and pat face dry.
Enjoy fresh radiant skin.

For The Lips   Lip balm for Tamar

Honey Citrus Lip Gloss (Spa Index)

7-8 tsp. sweet almond oil
2-tsp. beeswax
1-Vitamin E capsule
1-tsp. honey
5-drops citrus flavoring or essential oil (we like lime)
Microwave-safe container with lid
Cosmetic / balm container with lid

Melt the sweet almond oil and beeswax together in the microwave safe
container for 1-2 minutes. Remove the mixture from the microwave,
and pierce the vitamin E capsule with a pin or tip of a knife, and squirt
into mixture. Whisk the contents of the Vitamin E capsule, honey, and
flavoring, into the oil mixture, continuing to whisk until set. Spoon your
new lip-gloss into a small, balm container with tight lid.

emon Lip Gloss (Spa Index)

1-tsp honey
1-Tbsp vitamin E oil
1-tsp. of Aloe Vera gel
2-tsp of grated beeswax
1-Tbsp pure almond extract
6-Drops of lemon essential oil

Melt beeswax, remove from heat and while constantly stirring - Add honey, Aloe Vera, almond extract, vitamin E. Add the lemon essential oil last.

Easy Lip Balm Recipe - using Lanolin

1oz. Olive Oil
.3oz of Lanolin
.4oz of Shea Butter
. 4oz of Beeswax
Flavor oil for taste

Melt beeswax gently in the microwave. In a separate container, heat the Lanolin oil and Shea Butter until it is liquefied. Add the olive oil to the melted Lanolin oil and Shea Butter. Add beeswax to the oil, slowly, stirring completely. Add flavoring (if desired) and pour into containers.

TIP: Any lip-gloss or balm can become colored by adding zinc oxide and/or lip safe mica. If you use just mica, you will have a sheer lipstick. The zinc oxide makes it more matte. Experiment with colors. You can find retailers at the end of this section.

Cranberry Lip Gloss (Honey Board)

Protect sensitive lips from the drying winter elements with this simple yet rich lip balm. Delightful to wear alone or on top of your lipstick for extra shine!

1-Tablespoon sweet almond oil
10-fresh cranberries
1-teaspoon honey
1-drop vitamin E oil

Mix all the ingredients together in a microwave-safe bowl. Microwave for two minutes or until the mixture just begins to boil. (Bowl may also be heated in a pan of water on a stovetop). Stir well and gently crush the berries. Cool mixture for five minutes and then strain through a fine sieve to remove all the fruit pieces. Stir again and set aside to cool completely. When cool, transfer into a small portable plastic container or tin.   Apply a small amount onto your lips and remember to smile!

For The Hair

Beer Hair Rinse (Spa Index)

1-oz distilled or clean catch rain water
2-teaspoons apple cider vinegar
7-drops lemon essential oil
1-ounce beer (stale works fine)
5-drops rosemary essential oil
5-drops calendula essential oil (optional, but recommended for blondes)

Mix all ingredients together. Use as a final rinse, rinse well. Beer adds protein to make hair shiny and make it feel thicker.

Cucumber Hair Drench (Spa Index)

If you swim in a chlorinated pool for exercise on a regular basis, the same damage you've noticed happening to your skin and bathing suit, is happening to your hair, as well. Try this treatment at home to keep chlorine damage to a minimum.

1-egg
1 half-eggshell's worth of olive oil (i.e., one portion of the eggshell you broke apart)
1-quarter of a peeled cucumber

Blend the egg, olive oil and peeled cucumber in a blender or food processor until smooth. Spread evenly through your hair, leave on for 10 minutes, and then thoroughly rinse. For the best results year-round, continue this treatment monthly.

Chamomile Shampoo

1 ½-cups distilled water
4-bags of Chamomile tea (or 1 handful of fresh Chamomile flowers)
4-tablespoons pure soap flakes
1 ½-tablespoons glycerin

Steep the tea bags in 1-½ cups of boiled water for about 10 minutes. Remove the tea bags and add the soap flakes to the water. Stir occasionally. Once the soap has softened, stir in glycerin until the mixture is well blended. Pour into a bottle. Store in a dark corner of your refrigerator. Will last about a week.

Dry Shampoo

½-cup cornstarch
Sprinkle the cornstarch in your hair, let it absorb for a few minutes, brush it out. This is great if you are in a pinch.

Herbal Shampoo

2-cups distilled water
1 ½-tablespoons dried soapwart root (chopped)
2-teaspoons dried lemon verbena
2-teaspoons dried rosemary

Bring water to a boil and then add the soapwart. Simmer and cover for about 20 minutes. Remove from heat, stir in the herbs and allow mixture to cool. Strain the mixture, keeping the liquid. Pour into a bottle. Store in a dark corner of your refrigerator. Must be used within 8-10 days.

Rosemary Honey Hair Conditioner (Honey board)

½-cup honey
¼-cup warmed olive oil or 2 Tablespoons for normal to oily hair
4-drops essential oil of rosemary
1-teaspoon xanthum gum (available in health food stores)

Place all the ingredients in a small bowl and mix thoroughly. Pour into a clean plastic bottle with a tight fitting stopper or lid. Apply a small amount at a time to slightly dampened hair. Massage scalp and work mixture through hair until completely coated. Cover hair with a warm towel (towel can be heated in a microwave or dryer) or shower cap; leave on for 30 minutes to fully nourish and condition your hair. Remove towel or shower cap; shampoo lightly and rinse with cool water. Dry as normal and enjoy shinier, softer and healthier hair the natural way.

Deep Conditioner

½-cup of real mayonnaise (consider making your own!) – make sure it's ✓ not salad dressing

Comb the mayonnaise through your damp hair. Then wrap your head in a towel, and let it penetrate for 20 minutes. Shampoo.

Hair Dye

This is a bit more complicated, so I reference you to www.hennapage.com. Henna is a plant-derived powder that is commonly used in non-permanent tattoos. It is easy to use, and can achieve subtle and drastic color changes. Henna is easy to use, long lasting, and can achieve both subtle and dramatic changes in hair color. Make sure you purchase pure, tattoo quality henna to get the best results. Tip: Henna mixes sold in boxes in stores are usually ineffective and often contain the same chemicals as toxic dyes.

Homemade Hair Spray

Chop one lemon (or an orange for dry hair). Place in a pot with 2 cups water. Boil until half of the initial amount remains. Cool, strain, and place in a spray bottle. Store in the refrigerator. If it is too sticky, add more water. Add one ounce rubbing alcohol as a preservative and then the spray can be stored for up to two weeks unrefrigerated. **Warning: lemon juice can lighten hair!

Homemade Hair Gel

½ to 1-teaspoon unflavored gelatin
1-cup warm water

Dissolve gelatin in 1-cup warm water. Keep refrigerated and use as you would a purchased gel. Add essential oils for scent.

Hair Shine (Honey Board)

1-teaspoon honey
4-cups warm water
Lemon (for blondes and light brunettes as it lightens color)

Stir honey into warm water. Blondes may wish to add a squeeze of lemon. After shampooing pour mixture through hair. Do not rinse out. Dry as normal.

An Eco-Babe Tip:
I usually rinse my hair with lemon tea once a month to add blonde highlights. Lemon not only lightens hair, but it's also very drying, so I wouldn't recommend using something like this more frequently. I've developed my hair rinse to bring out both the blonde and red in my hair. I boil about 16-20 ounces of water. Then, I add two tea bags: one chamomile and one rose hips. Next, I squeeze 1/2 of a lemon into the tea and drop it in. I cover the mixture and leave it overnight. In the morning, I squeeze the lemon again. After showering, I rinse my hair with it. Cover your eyes with a towel while pouring it over your hair. Also, the bathtub will be slippery from all of the lemon oil. So be careful getting out of the tub or shower! For medium-dark brunettes, forget the chamomile tea, and add extra rose hips tea leaves. **– Nina Ricci, English Teacher, South Korea**

For The Hands and Feet

Beach Sand Foot Scrub (Spa Index)

2-Tablespoons Canola oil
2-Tablespoons dry beach sand
3-5 drops rosemary oil

When going to the beach, take a small vial of the liquid ingredients with you. Once at the beach, use an empty container (a soda cup is fine) to mix the ingredients together. Mix into a paste. Massage sand scrub onto feet (and elbows), concentrating especially on problem areas. Rinse off in the foamy waves; pat dry with your beach towel.

Apricot Oil-Lanolin Cuticle Cream (Spa Index)

½-tsp apricot kernel or emu oil

2-tsp lanolin

1-drop essential oil of your choice (optional)

Melt oils together, add essential oil, pour into jar or small pots and let set. To use, massage into cuticles.

Cuticle Softener (Spa Index)

1-tsp. olive oil

1-tsp. vitamin E oil

Combine and massage into nails and cuticles.

Peppermint Honey Feet Treat (Honey Board)

Makes 2 treatments.

4-Tbsp. aloe vera gel

4-tsp. grated beeswax

2-tsp. honey

2-tsp. fresh mint, optional

6-drops peppermint essential oil

2-drops arnica oil

2-drops camphor oil

2-drops eucalyptus oil

Rinse mint leaves and place on a paper towel to dry. Grind mint using coffee grinder (or by hand using mortar and pestle). Set aside. Melt beeswax using a small double boiler. In a microwave safe glass bowl combine aloe vera and honey, mix well. Stir in beeswax. Let cool. Add mint and oils stirring until completely mixed. Apply after bath or shower to entire feet and toes. Store remaining feet treat in covered in cool place away from sun or heat.

For The Bath

Aromatic Milk Bath (Spa Index)

Use this mixed concoction immediately after making it, for soft and silky skin.

1-egg
½-cup light olive oil
1-tablespoon glycerin
½-cup dried milk powder
1-drop jasmine essential oil
1-drop rose essential oil
6-drops lavender essential oil
2-cups distilled water

Beat together egg, olive oil, glycerin and milk powder with a whisk or hand held beater. While beating add essential oils. Continue beating until a smooth paste forms. Add the water a little at a time, continuing to beat. Immediately add to your warm drawn bath (be careful...if the water is too hot you'll make scrambled eggs).

Bath Cookies (Spa Index)

Our most requested recipe!

2-cups finely ground sea salt
½-cup baking soda
½-cup cornstarch
2-Tbsp light oil
1-tsp vitamin E oil
2-eggs
5-6-drops essential oil of your choice

Preheat your oven to 350 F. Combine all the listed ingredients and form into a dough. Using a teaspoon or so of dough at a time, roll it gently in the palm of your hand until it forms a ball. Form all dough into one-teaspoon balls, and gently place them on an ungreased cookie sheet. Consider sprinkling the bath balls with herbs, flower petals, cloves, citrus zest and similar aromatic ingredients. Bake your bath cookies for ten minutes, until they are lightly browned. Do not over bake. Allow the bath cookies to cool completely. To use, drop 1 or 2 cookies into a warm bath and allow to dissolve. Yield: 24 cookies, enough for 12 baths.

Foaming Vanilla Honey Bath (Honey Board)

Banish the winter blahs and dissolve away the harshness of the day by relaxing in a soothing bath. Honey is nature's silky moisturizer and guaranteed to sweeten your mood!

1-cup sweet almond oil, light olive or sesame oil may be substituted
½-cup honey
½-cup liquid soap
1-Tablespoon vanilla extract

Measure the oil into a medium bowl, and then carefully stir in remaining ingredients until mixture is fully blended. Pour into a clean plastic bottle with a tight-fitting stopper or lid. Shake gently before using. Enough for four large luxurious baths. Swirl desired amount into the bathtub under running water. Then step in and descend into a warm, silky escape.

Champagne Bubble Bath (Spa Index)

¼-Cup foaming concentrate
¾-Cup distilled water
½-tsp. table salt (do not use sea salt)
1-tablespoon glycerin
¼-tsp. champagne or white wine fragranced oil
Melted votive candle

Buy a bottle of champagne. Enjoy the contents, but save the bottle! Heat water (not boiling just hot), stir in foaming concentrate and glycerin until completely dissolved. Add champagne or wine fragrance oil and stir well. Add salt, stirring until dissolved. Allow mixture to cool. If it is not as thick as you would like, add another 1/4 tsp. salt stirring until dissolved. Pour into a clean champagne bottle and cork. When firmly corked, dip cork into melted votive wax, sealing the bottle closed. Present as a gift.

For Special Needs

Hair Remover – Body Sugaring (Spa Index)
Juice of 1/2 a lemon
1-cup sugar
1/4-cup honey
Cornstarch
Clean cloth cotton strips
Wooden stick or spreader

Dust the area to be waxed, with cornstarch. Combine the first three ingredients in a clean glass bowl, and microwave for two minutes. Stop and stir your sugar mixture every 20-30 seconds. Let it cool to a comfortable warmth, and, using a wooden stick, spread a very thin layer onto your clean skin. Immediately cover the mixture with a strip of cotton fabric. Briskly stroke the strip several times *in the direction* of the hair growth, and then, pull the skin taut, and quickly rip away the cotton strip, *against the direction* of hair growth. As you proceed, you may need to reheat your sugar mixture in the microwave to keep it warm. Do not boil it or overheat as you could easily burn your skin.

Moist Towelettes (Spa Index)

20 to 24-Squares of white heavy-duty quality paper towels

1-cup witch hazel

1-teaspoon glycerin

1-3-drops of essential oil of your choice

Combine the witch hazel, glycerin, and essential oil. Mix well and set aside. Next, separate and stack each of the paper towel squares from the roll. Then cut each square in half. You will now have rectangles. Fold each rectangle into thirds as if you would a letter. Now, fold each in half as if you were closing a book. Holding the stack of towels firmly closed, place in a pie pan and hold down with your finger. Pour witch hazel mixture over towels. Let stand for a few minutes to absorb all of the liquid. Stack towels in an empty lidded plastic container or zip-lock type bag. Keep in your car, bathroom, gym locker or other useful places.

After shave (Spa Index)

¼-cup witch hazel

½-cup distilled water

1-tbsp olive oil

½-cup dried herbs or zest (lavender flowers, chamomile, rosemary, sage, or citrus zests) and/or a few drops of your choice essential oils: consider rosemary, lavender, sage, eucalyptus, cedar, juniper, cinnamon, or clove. Cedar and sage makes a wonderful combination, according to our male staff members.

Combine ingredients in a glass jar. Cover and place in a dark fairly cool place to steep. Shake the jar once or twice a day. Repeat this process for two to three weeks. Strain out the added products, and store the after-shave in a spray bottle or other bottle.

Athlete's Foot Treatment (Spa Index)

20 to 30-garlic cloves, minced
2 to 4-tsp. ground cinnamon
2 to 4-tsp. powdered cloves
5 oz. 100-proof vodka

Add garlic, cinnamon, and cloves to vodka in a dark-colored glass jar or bottle with lid. Seal tightly. Store out of direct sunlight for two weeks, shaking to mix every few days. The tincture will be ready to use in 14 days.   To treat athlete's foot, use cotton balls or a cloth to apply the tincture to the entire sole of the foot as well as between all the toes. Apply twice a day, morning and night. Let dry, and then dust the entire foot with cornstarch. If a rash or any unusual irritation develops, discontinue using Athlete's Foot Treatment. If, after having used this treatment for two weeks and athlete's foot symptoms continue, consult your physician.

Sunblock (Spa Index)

Did you know the active ingredients in sunblock often dissipate after the season? So, always use a sunblock, but don't purchase in bulk or save that last little bit in the bottle for next season. Buy as you go, in order to always have a fresh batch, or, make your own. Most conventional sunblocks have toxic ingredients. See "Shopping Organically."
Note: This recipe will leave a white nose "lifeguard style."

1-Tbsp zinc oxide
1 and ½-tsp light sesame oil
1-Tbsp rosewater

Mix together the zinc oxide and sesame oil. Heat the mixture gently, using a double boiler, and stir well to mix. Remove from heat and slowly add the rosewater, as you continue stirring. Allow to cool completely, and store in a clean container with a tight lid, in the fridge. Yield: 2 oz. Keeps: Up to 10 days in the fridge.

Don't Bug Me Insect Repellent (Spa Index)

2-cup witch hazel
1 and ½-teaspoon citronella essential oil
1-Tablespoon apple cider vinegar
Combine into a 16 oz spray bottle. Shake vigorously before using.
Requires no refrigeration. Apply liberally.

Insect Repellent Lotion

Add a few drops of citronella essential oil to your favorite organic
lotion, mix well and apply.

Scented Rocks Potpourri (Spa Index)

½-cup plain flour
½-cup salt
¼-tsp. essential oil
2/3-cups boiling water
Food coloring, if desired
Glitter or other "mix-ins" as desired

In bowl, mix all dry ingredients well. Add your favorite essential oil and
boiling water to dry ingredients. (The scent will be strong, but will fade
slightly when your rocks dry.) For colored stones, blend in food
coloring, one drop at a time, until desired shade is reached. Blend
ingredients and form roughly shaped stones. Allow stones to dry. Place
scent stones in a bowl or dish to scent a room, or try in the ashtray of
your vehicle.

Resources

Make your own cosmetics (www.Makingcosmetics.com)
Cosmetic Database (www.Cosmeticsdatabase.com)
Organic Consumers (www.Organicconsumers.org).
Safe Cosmetics Database (www.Safecosmetics.org)
Spa Index (www.Spaindex.com)
The Honey Board (www.Honey.com)
Learn how to make soap (www.Teachsoap.com/easycpsoap.html)

Bombeli, Karin and Thomas Bombeli (2007) Recipes for Color
　　　Cosmetics (Vol. 1 from the Series: Make Your Own Cosmetics!)
　　　(Make Your Own Cosmetics!)
Cavitch, Susan Miller. (1997). *The SoapMakers Companion*
Failor, Catherine. (2000). *Making Natural Liquid Soaps: Herbal Shower
　　　Gels / Conditioning Shampoos / Moisturizing Hand Soaps*
Farrer-Halls , Gill (2006) Natural Beauty Recipe Book: How to Make
　　　Your Own Organic Cosmetics and Beauty Products
Gabriel, Julie (2008) The Green Beauty Guide: Your Essential Resource
　　　to Organic and Natural Skin Care, Hair Care, Makeup, and
　　　Fragrances
Makela, Casey. (1997). *Milk-Based Soaps: Making Natural, Skin-
　　　Nourishing Soap*
Morris, Janita and Juanita Morris. (2000). *The Soapmaker: Natural
　　　Handmade Soap from Your Kitchen*
Nelson, Maxine (2005) Creative Faces: Make Your Own Makeup

Sun screen.

The Yummy Tummy

Now that we babes are looking and smelling hot, it's time to focus on our diets. When I use the word diet, I'm not using it in the 'starve to death' way most people think it means. Diet means the food or beverages someone consumes. It has nothing to do with losing weight unless you want it to. In other words, a heart healthy diet or pregnancy diet is a form of a diet. No matter what type of diet you are on, it is important to buy organic foods. If you've read the previous sections, you know how bad chemicals, pesticides, and herbicides are, so choose organic to keep yourself and the planet healthy. Read "The Cheaper Organic" later in this section, for more information about organic food. The best are locally grown seasonal foods. This way you are not paying for your food to be shipped from the opposite end of the planet. You will find farmers market and co-op resources at the end of this chapter.

If you retain anything from this chapter, I hope it includes this. Overall, for a healthy diet, try to eat seasonal foods, locally grown foods, organic foods and whole foods. Keep that in mind the next time you go shopping.

I want to take just a moment to talk about some of the green diets that are popular right now. This is by no means meant to be a complete guide to each diet. Check out the books and resources for more information.

The Raw Food Diet
What is the Raw Food Diet?
The raw food diet is a diet based on the belief that cooking diminishes the nutritional value of food. It consists of unprocessed and uncooked plant foods, such as fresh fruit and vegetables, sprouts, seeds, nuts, grains, and dried fruit. I will go into a deeper list later. You can't cook food above 116°F, because it is believed to destroy the enzymes in the food that are necessary for proper digestion and absorption of the food. Typically, at least 75% of the diet must be living or raw.

What are the Benefits of the Raw Food Diet?
There are many benefits for a Raw Food Diet because it contains fewer bad fats (trans and saturated) and is lower in sodium than a typical American diet. It is also high in potassium, magnesium, folate, and fiber, all of which are associated with a reduced risk of heart disease, diabetes and cancer, as well as lower cholesterol. While I found no specific studies promoting this, proponents of the raw food diet believe it increases energy, improves skin health, aids in digestion and leads to weight loss.

What can I eat?
Unprocessed, preferably organic, whole foods such as:
Fresh fruits and vegetables
Nuts
Seeds
Beans
Grains
Legumes
Dried fruit
Seaweed
Unprocessed organic or natural foods
Freshly juiced fruit and vegetables
Purified water
Young coconut milk
How do I eat it?
Sprouting seeds, grains, and beans
Juicing fruit and vegetables
Soaking nuts and dried fruit
Blending
Dehydrating food

Are there any Side Effects?
Some people experience a reaction similar to detoxification, the symptoms of which depend on what the previous diet was like. Symptoms can last for several days and include cravings, nausea and

headaches. In fact the diet is not suggested for certain people including children, pregnant or nursing women, people with anemia and people at risk for osteoporosis. This is due to the fact that it is difficult and time consuming to ensure that all nutritional needs are met. This diet is associated with the following nutritional deficiencies: Calcium, Iron, B12, Protein, and Calories. (However, vitamin deficiencies are rampant in Western diets, whether you eat greasy French fries or fresh fruit.)

What do the critics say?
Some dispute the science behind the raw food diet. While some enzymes are deactivated when food is heated, some (phytochemicals such as beta-carotene) are made easier to absorb with heat. In addition, the body uses its own enzymes for digestion, so they believe it doesn't really matter how you cook food.

BARF Diet

Your pets can get on a raw food diet too! BARF stands for "biologically appropriate raw food" or "Bones and Raw Food." According to Barfworld.com "the BARF Diet mimics the way your pet used to eat before highly processed, grain-based foods entered our pet's food chain." For more information, check out the resources.

Resources:

Boutenko, Sergei and Valya Boutenko. *Fresh: The Ultimate Live-Food Cookbook*
Boutenko, Victoria. *Green for Life*
Brotman, Juliano and Erika Lenkert. *Raw: The Uncook Book: New Vegetarian Food for Life*
Cornblee, Jennifer. *Raw Food Made Easy For 1 or 2 People*
Winters, Christine. *The Magic of Raw: A Guided Tour of the Raw Foods Diet and Lifestyle*

Alissa Cohen (www.Alissacohen.com)

Living Foods (www.Living-foods.com/faq.html)
Raw Guru (www.Rawguru.com)
We Like It Raw (www.Welikeitraw.com)

BARF:
Bailey, Sandra. *Real Dogs Don't Eat Kibble! (Naturally Healthy Dog)*
Flaim, Denise and Michael W. Fox. *The Holistic Dog Book: Canine
	Care for the 21st Century*
Lonsdale, Tom. *Work Wonders: Feed Your Dog Raw Meaty Bones*
Macdonald, Carina Beth. *Raw Dog Food: Make It Easy for You and
	Your Dog*

NJ Boxers (www.Njboxers.com/faqs.htm)
Raw on Wiko (En.wikipedia.org/wiki/Raw_feeding)
Barf World (www.Barfworld.com)
Aunt Jeni (www.Auntjeni.com/barf.htm)

The Vegetarian/Vegan Diet

What is the Vegetarian Diet?

There are four types of Vegetarians. Depending on how strict the diet is
it excludes a combination of meat, game, slaughter by-products, and
possibly poultry, fish, eggs, diary products and honey.
	Lacto-ovo-vegetarian: This diet includes dairy products, eggs, and
		plant foods.
	Lacto-vegetarian: This diet includes dairy products and plant foods.
	Ovo-vegetarian: This diet includes eggs and plant foods.
	Vegan (VEE-gun): This diet includes only plant foods.

What are the Benefits of the Vegetarian Diet?
The benefits are similar to the Raw Food Diet. Many scientific studies
have shown that a properly planned vegetarian diet can significantly
lower risks of cancer, heart disease, and other diseases. Proponents also
tout increased energy, better digestion and weight loss.

What can I eat?

The most common answer to that question is "Anything We Want!" GoVeg.com writes, "There are vegetarian alternatives to almost any animal food, from soy sausages and "Fib Ribs" to Tofurky jerky and mock lobster. Vegetarian-friendly menus are sprouting up everywhere— even Burger King offers veggie burgers—and more and more eateries are focusing exclusively on vegetarian and vegan foods. There are fantastic alternatives to every dairy product you can imagine, including Soy Delicious ice cream, Silk chocolate soy milk, Tofutti cream cheese, and more." I personally prefer the flavor of soymilk, cheese, lunch "meat" and ice cream, to the conventional.

How do I eat it?

There are no changes in preparation of foods, except you might want to study up on herbs and spices if you find vegetables tend to have a plain flavor.

Are there any Side Effects?

There is a chance that you do not receive enough nutrients on a vegetarian diet. Common deficiencies include vitamin B12, calcium, iron, vitamin D, zinc, and omega-3 fatty acids. Talk to a dietician if you do not eat eggs and milk, especially if you are pregnant or breast-feeding. According to some pregnancy books, soy can make it difficult to conceive, so if you are trying to get pregnant, talk to your doctor or nutritionist.

What do the critics say?

Critics often attack vegetarians in a personal manner, as if the fact that they do not eat meat is an affront. Ignoring that, other critics fault this diet for nutritional reasons. Some think that a vegetarian diet is incomplete because it does not include protein from meat. However, vegetarians rarely find themselves short on protein as it can be found in abundance in grains, legumes, soy foods and dairy products. Critics also mention that the only way to get vitamin B12 is through meat. For this reason, vegetarians must take a supplement or eat B12-fortified foods.

There is also a deficiency of calcium in a vegan diet. There are other so-called deficiencies, but these are easily addressed by spending some time in the sun (vitamin D), and taking a multi-vitamin.

Resources:

Barnard, M.D., Neal. *Eat Right, Live Longer*
Eisnitz , Gail. *Slaughterhouse: The Shocking Story of Greed, Neglect, and Inhumane Treatment Inside the U.S. Meat Industry*
Esselstyn, Dr. Caldwell. *Prevent and Reverse Heart Disease*
Davis, Karen. *Prisoned Chickens, Poisoned Eggs*
Marcus, Erik. *Vegan: The New Ethics of Eating*
Pavlina, Erin. *Raising Vegan Children in a Non-Vegan World*

Go Veg (www.Goveg.com)
Veg Source (www.Vegsource.com)
PETA (www.Peta.org or www.peta2.com)
Veg Family (www.Vegfamily.com)

The Cheaper Organic

For those of you who cannot afford to go 100% organic (me too!) there is a solution. Have you ever heard of the "Dirty Dozen?" These are the foods that have the highest concentration of pesticides, chemicals, hormones and additives. If you focus your organic spending on these twelve, you are eliminating a large proportion of toxins from your diet[25]. Foods in parenthesis are also known to contain a lot of pesticides, but didn't quite make the dirty dozen. For a great shopping guide, visit http://foodnews.org/walletguide.php.

There are three levels of organic certification by the USDA.

100% Organic – This means that product is all organic.

Organic – This means that the product contains 95% organic ingredients.

Made with Organic Ingredients – This means that the product contains at least 70% organic ingredients.

The green and white USDA logo can only be found on 100% organic and organic products. Just like beauty products, avoid products that claim to be "pure," "natural," "enriched," or "made with real fruit/whole grains." When they use phrases like that, they are just trying to look healthy.

1. Meat (Eggs). The greatest danger with meat comes from the process of feeding/raising the animal, rather than the animal itself. Factor in the pesticides on the grain fed to the animals and the hormones/antibiotics given to the animals, and you get a large quantity of chemicals that are dangerous if they enter the environment. The only option for those who must eat is to purchase USDA Certified Organic meat. This standard is given only to animals that are fed organic grain and receive no hormones and antibiotics. Organic, grass-fed beef is leaner, and contains five times more omega-3 fats, which are good for the heart.

Of course, the greenest option is to wean off of livestock meats entirely. There are other environmental factors that are at play here. Livestock gas (including cow farts) account for 18 percent of all greenhouse gas emissions. The U.S. Department of Agriculture (USDA) reports that the American meat industry produces more than 1.3 billion tons of waste annually — five tons for every U.S. citizen and 130 times the volume of human waste[26]. Livestock also require an enormous amount of land that could otherwise be used to grow crops for human consumption or forestation. According to EVLiving.com:

> Grazing [land] occupies an incredible 26 percent of the ice- and water-free surface (arable land) of the planet Earth. The area devoted to growing crops to feed those animals amounts to 33 percent of arable land… And food grown for animals could be feeding people. Raising livestock consumes 90 percent of the soy

76

crop in the U.S., 80 percent of its corn and 70 percent of its grain… Livestock production consumes eight percent of the world's water (mainly to irrigate animal feed); causes 55 percent of land erosion and sediment; uses 37 percent of all pesticides; directly or indirectly results in 50 percent of all antibiotic use; and dumps a third of all nitrogen and phosphorous into our fresh water supplies.

So, now that you're feeling a little guilty about the cheeseburger you ate the other day, don't despair. If you seriously want to green your diet, you can replace meat protein with the much healthier (and cheaper) alternatives of beans, nuts, and soy. Try Tofurky® and Boca Burgers®!

2. Milk. Pesticides and other man-made chemicals are found just about everywhere, including our milk, human and cow. Current studies show that when pesticides are found in milk, they are found in small quantities. You need to consider how much you consume because that small amount of pesticides can become significant if milk is a large portion of your diet. Studies also show that the hormones contained in milk can cause puberty to start earlier in children. So be wary of giving non-organic to children. However, there is an organic option. The USDA organic standard is given only to animals that are fed organic grain and receive no hormones and antibiotics. You can even go one step further and try to buy local milk.

An even better alternative is to switch to organic soymilk. It is a little bit more expensive than milk, lower in cholesterol, higher in protein and has considerably more fiber than cow's milk. The only downside is that it has less calcium than milk. Take a calcium supplement. I personally love it for the flavor! Silk soymilk comes in several flavors from plain, vanilla, very vanilla, and chocolate. Other milk alternatives include: rice milk, coconut milk, almond milk, and tofu buttermilk.

3. Coffee. Look for the Fair Trade Certified Organic label on your coffee. This is the only way you can be sure that your coffee does not have chemicals or pesticides in it. The label also means that the farms and workers who grew/packaged your coffee were paid a fair wage and were treated fairly. It will be your way of fighting sweatshop labor and saving the environment!

4. Peaches (Nectarines). These delicate fruits are regularly treated with multiple pesticides. The soft skins allow the pesticides to reach the inside. Can't find organic? Safer alternatives: watermelon, tangerines, oranges and grapefruit.

Important tip: For fruits/veggies that you cut through to get to the 'meat' inside like melons, squashes, and cucumbers, you still need to wash the outside. As you cut through them, pesticides and bacteria can be transferred into the meat. This is partly what caused the E. coli outbreak in 2008.

5. Apples, applesauce, apple juice (Pears). Scrubbing and peeling doesn't eliminate chemical residue completely so it's best to buy organic when it comes to apples. Peeling a fruit or vegetable also strips away many of their beneficial nutrients. Organic apples contain more disease fighting nutrients than non-organic. Can't find organic? Safer alternatives: watermelon, bananas and tangerines.

6. Sweet bell peppers. These vegetables are regularly treated with multiple pesticides. The soft skins allow the pesticides to reach the inside. Can't find organic? Safer alternatives: green peas, broccoli and cabbage.

7. Celery. Celery has no protective skin, which makes it almost impossible to wash off the chemicals that are used on conventional crops. Can't find organic? Safer alternatives: broccoli, radishes and onions.

8. Strawberries (Cherries). If you buy strawberries out of season, they're most likely imported from countries that use less-stringent regulations for pesticide use. Try to buy local and in season. Can't find organic? Safer alternatives: blueberries, kiwi and pineapples.

9. Lettuces (Spinach). Leafy greens are frequently contaminated with what are considered the most potent pesticides used on food. Can't find organic? Safer alternatives: cabbage, cauliflower and Brussels sprouts.

10. Grapes. Imported grapes run a much greater risk of contamination than those grown domestically. Vineyards can be sprayed with different pesticides during different growth periods of the grape, and no amount of washing or peeling will eliminate contamination because of the grape's thin skin. Try to buy local and in season. Can't find organic? Safer alternatives: blueberries, kiwi and raspberries.

11. Potatoes. Potatoes rank high for pesticide residue. It also gets fungicides added to the soil for growing. Studies show that 81% of potatoes still contain pesticides after being washed and peeled. Can't find organic? Safer alternatives: eggplant, cabbage and earthy mushrooms.

12. Tomatoes. These delicate fruits are regularly treated with multiple pesticides. The soft skins allow the pesticides to reach the inside. Can't find organic? Safer alternatives: green peas, broccoli and asparagus.

If you can't find organic products in your grocery store, you can request them by talking or writing to the manager. If that doesn't work, try purchasing your goods from local co-ops, farmers markets, farms, or on the internet.

I am a big fan of coupons. There are several coupon websites on the Internet. Check those out to see if there are any coupons for organic foods. If you can purchase them with coupons, they will probably be cheaper than the non-organic version. You can also go directly to the manufactures website, and they usually have coupons for their new products. Don't forget to also check your Sunday paper.

With today's gas prices being as high as they are, I don't recommend comparison-shopping in person. Instead of going to the store to check their prices, go to their websites and compare the ads. Once you know what products you will buy from each store, make a list and map out your route for gas efficiency. You can also purchase organic food in bulk to save money.

I LOVE farmer's market and try to go as often as I can. You can find organic produce there that is often cheaper than grocery stores. Remember to visit the ATM first, as most venders don't take credit or debit cards. Visit **www.localharvest.org** to find local markets.

You can also join a co-op or purchasing/buying club. These are often cheaper than farmer's markets, because everything is purchased in bulk at wholesale prices. In a buying club, you place your order, along with everyone in the club. Then that one bulk order is made and you pick up your stuff from whoever is organizing. I found several in my area on Yahoo and Google groups.

Resources:

Check out The Daily Green's top-ten list of fruit and vegetables you don't need to buy organic, with tips for buying and how to clean, store and use them in delicious recipes.
http://www.thedailygreen.com/healthy-eating/eat-safe/Save-On-Sustainable-Foods

The information for this section in regard to pesticides in fruits and vegetables is based on The Environmental Working Group's analysis of federal pesticide testing data for commonly eaten fruits and vegetables.
http://www.foodnews.org/release.php

Burke, Cindy. *To Buy or Not to Buy Organic: What You Need to Know to Choose the Healthiest, Safest, Most Earth-Friendly Food*
Joachim, David and Rochelle Davi. *Fresh Choices: More than 100 Easy Recipes for Pure Food When You Can't Buy 100% Organic*
Waters, Alice, Anne Gatti, Daphne Lambert, and Erica Bower. *Slice of Organic Life*

CSA (www.csacenter.org)
Diamond Organics (www.diamondorganics.com)
EV Living (www.Evliving.com)
Fresh Direct (www.freshdirect.com)
Green Feet (www.Greenfeet.net/newsletter/eatorganic.shtml)
Green People (www.Greenpeople.org/HomeDelivery.html) - Co-op
    and buying club directory
Listing of Farmers markets (www.ams.usda)
Local Harvest (www.localharvest.org)
Organic Consumers
    (www.Organicconsumers.org/organic/natfrugal012306.cfm)
Organic Consumers Buying Guide
    (www.Organicconsumers.org/btc/BuyingGuide.cfm)
Planet Friendly (www.Planetfriendly.net/organic.html)
SLOW Food International (www.slowfood.com)
SPUD (www.spud.com) – Small Potatoes Urban Delivery
Trader Joe's (www.traderjoes.com)
U.S. Dept of Agriculture National Organic Program (www.ams.usda)
U.S. Dept of Agriculture Nutrition Information (www.nutrition.gov)

Foods to Avoid

Partially Hydrogenated Fats/Oils and "Trans Fats" – These are the fats that are bad for you and your heart. Some margarine contains this, as well as fast foods. Better alternatives include olive oil, organic and partially hydrogenated/trans fat free margarine, extra-virgin cold-pressed olive oil, grapeseed oil, coconut oil and real organic butter.

Quality oils will be slightly cloudy, as they still have their nutrients intact and haven't been over processed. Also look for cold-processed and unfiltered oils.

High-Fructose Corn Syrup – Many scientists and doctors believe that corn syrup is responsible for obesity in the United States. Corn syrup is a cheap sweetener that can be found in everything from candies and cakes, to rice and bread. Even foods that we think are healthy contain corn syrup. So read the labels. High-fructose corn syrup is chemically processed and in many cases genetically engineered.

Other ingredients that are made from genetically engineered corn include xanthan gum, fructose, sorbitol, mannitol, citric acid, lactic acid, maltodextrin, glucose, and MSG.

Refined Sugars – Once again, food manufacturers take something good and process it, add chemicals to it and basically beat it up until it is unidentifiable. Refined sugars are striped down versions of sugar cane and sugar beets. They remove all nutrients from it. These sugars are terrible for diabetics, rot teeth, and can lead to heart disease, cancer, depression, obesity, and high blood pressure.

Better alternatives include organic sugar, stevia (super sweet), organic honey, barley malt syrup and agave syrup (safe for diabetics).

Regular Iodized Salt – Once again, iodized salt is a stripped down version of something that was once healthy. It has no minerals and is linked with high blood pressure. A better alternative is the very tasty and healthy sea salt.

Fish – I'm not saying to avoid all fish, but there are some that you should think twice about. We are over-fishing our oceans and devastating our environment, so we should try to eat the most sustainable fish we can. There is a great sustainable seafood guide at **www.eartheasy.com.** For a quick reference, I have listed the fish that you should avoid based on the health of the wild population, how it's caught and the impact eating it has on the environment.

Alaska king crab	Farmed Scottish	Orange roughy
Atlantic cod	salmon	Red snapper
Atlantic halibut	Grouper	Skate
Bluefin tuna	Haddock	Swordfish
Caviar	Imported or tiger	Turbot
Chilean seabass	prawns	Yellowtail flounder
	Monkfish	

Another concern with fish is the amount of mercury. If you are pregnant or underweight you should avoid:

Canned tuna	Largemouth bass	Shark
Gulf coast oysters	Marlin	Tilefish
Halibut	Pike walleye	Tuna steak
King mackerel	Sea bass	White croaker

Check out the mercury calculator at **www.gotmercury.org**. It will calculate your mercury risk based on your weight and the amount of fish that you plan on eating.

In addition, some fish should not be eaten when they are farm-raised or ocean-raised. This means they were raised in pens as opposed to caught in the wild. They are prone to disease and can negatively affect wild fish if they escape. Make sure you buy the following wild: salmon, tuna, halibut and snapper.

Recipes

RAW Food Recipes

Beet and Celery Salad by Kandace Brigleb*

Serves 4-6

This is a crunchy, Russian salad. I found this recipe in an old cookbook and worked with it in order to add in raw ingredients.

Ingredients

1 pound beets, peeled and grated

4 sticks of celery, finely chopped

2 tablespoons apple juice

1 tablespoon apple cider vinegar

4 scallions, finely chopped

2 tablespoons fresh parsley, chopped

3 tablespoons grapeseed oil

salt and pepper to taste

Directions

Mix beets and celery with apple juice.
In a separate bowl, whisk together the remaining ingredients.
Toss the celery/beets with half of the liquids. Then, drizzle the remaining liquid over the salad.
Chill for a couple hours and serve.

Lemon Cookies by Kandace Brigleb*

Makes 12 small cookies

Tart, chewy lemon macaroons. I'd recommend at least doubling this recipe, as the cookies are addictive and go quite fast!

Ingredients

1 cup cashews, soaked for 4 hours

zest of 1 lemon

½ cup fresh lemon juice, (approximately 2 lemons)

1 cup dry shredded coconut

¼ cup agave

Directions

Process cashews in food processor until they are pasty in consistency.
Mix in all other ingredients.
Place 1 tablespoon cookie dollops on a dehydrator sheet.
Dehydrate for approximately 12 hours at 105F *(could also dehydrate at 115F for 8-10 hours with similar result)*.
Enjoy!

Zucchini Ratatouille By Kandace Brigleb*
Serves 2

This is an easy recipe that goes great with a simple, tossed salad. The zucchini comes out of the dehydrator warm and there is something about the sauce that makes me swear that it has cheese in it. Great for when I'm craving a heartier dish.

Ingredients

2 large zucchini, cut into rounds

½ cup olive oil

2 tablespoons raw apple cider vinegar

1½ cups sun dried tomatoes

1 cup water as needed

2 tablespoons fresh thyme, minced

1 tablespoon fresh rosemary, minced

Celtic sea salt and pepper to taste

Directions

Cut zucchini into rounds using a knife or manoline. Toss zucchini in a mixing bowl with olive oil, salt and dash of pepper. Place zucchini on Teflex dehydrator sheets and dehydrate for 1 hour at 145F. Soak sun dried tomatoes with equal part water. At the end of an hour, blend the remaining ingredients in blender until smooth. Toss zucchini with sauce before serving.

*"Raw food has absolutely changed my life. Since August of 2006 I've been eating vegan and mostly raw. In that time, I've kicked the [hypoglycemia] that has been with me all my life, lost weight, and feel like a new person." --Kandace Brigleb, a partner at Needmore Designs, Portland, OR. (www.needmoredesigns.com). She has a blog at kandacerae.com.

Chocolate Cake
Serves 10

Ingredients
The Crust:
½-cup unsweetened cocoa powder
½-cup unsweetened carob
½-cup finely ground almonds
1/3-cup agave syrup
¼-cup coconut or cacao butter
Pinch of sea salt

The Filling:
2-cups unsweetened cocoa powder
1.5-cups agave syrup
1-cup coconut or cacao butter
1-Tbsp Vanilla extract

Directions
Begin with the crust. Combine all dry ingredients and sift. Slowly mix in the wet ingredients. Properly mixed, it will feel like dough. Press it into a 7-inch pan and chill in the refrigerator for an hour. After the crust has chilled for about 50 minutes, begin making the filling. Blend all of the ingredients in a blender until they are creamy smooth. Poor the mixture onto the crust and return it to the refrigerator for another hour. When you are ready to serve, decorate it with fresh berries or sliced oranges.

Portabella Mushroom Quiche

Based on a recipe by Rene Loux Underkoffler from Living Cuisine: The Art and Spirit of Raw Foods
Makes 6-8 servings

Ingredients

The Crust:
¾-cup whole buckwheat groats
3 cloves garlic
½-cup chopped red onion
½-cup chopped parsley
1-cup chopped carrot
1-cup chopped cabbage (Try bamboo shoots if you're adventurous!)
½-cup finely chopped walnuts (or your favorite nut. It tastes great with pistachios.)
1-Tbsp ground coriander seeds
Pinch of sundried sea salt
Pinch of fennel

The Mushrooms:
2 portabella mushrooms
3-Tbsp organic extra-virgin olive oil
2-Tbsp nama shoyu
2 cloves garlic, minced

The Filling:
½-cup whole cashews
¼-cup pine nuts
¼-cup lemon juice
2-Tbsp olive oil
2-Tbsp nama shoyu
3-Tbsp nutritional yeast
pinch sun-dried sea salt
3-cups chopped Swiss chard, arugula or spinach, take your pick
½-cup chopped basil

88

Directions:

Begin with the crust. Soak the buckwheat groats in two cups of water for about 3-8 hours. I find it's easy to set this up before I leave for work in the morning. Drain/strain/rinse several times until the water runs clear.

Finely chop the garlic, onion, parsley, carrots, cabbage and walnuts. If you have a food processor, this will immensely speed up the process. Mix will. Add the drained groats, ground coriander, sea salt and fennel and mix well. It should be a well mixed mash that you can easily press into a pie plate. Dehydrate at 108-110°F for 12-20 hours or until a crust forms. I find it's easiest to set this up before I go to bed, and then check on it in the morning.

After you put your crust in the dehydrator, it's time to prepare the portabella mushrooms. Rinse them off, remove the stems and cut them into thin slices. In a bowl, toss the sliced mushrooms with the olive oil, nama shoyu and garlic and allow it to marinate in the refrigerator overnight.

When the crust is formed, it's time to make the filing. Soak the cashews in one cup of water for about 30 minutes. Drain/strain/rinse. In your food processor, grind the drained cashews and pine nuts into a meal-like paste. Add the lemon juice, olive oil and nama shoyu and blend until creamy. Finally, add the yeast and sea salt and blend well. Put this mixture in a large bowl.

Get your mushrooms from the refrigerator and drain them. Save the juice. You will need to squeeze the excess moisture out of them. Add the mushrooms and basil to the cashews. Mix gently. Finally, gently fold in your Swiss chard, arugula or spinach. Spoon this mixture over the crust and let the entire thing set in the refrigerator for an hour before serving. This is optional, but I like to take the mushroom juice that I set aside and add a bit of flour to it to make a gravy-like paste. I then, smooth the paste on top of the quiche right before I eat it.

Parsnip-Pine Nut Whip (or Better than Mashed Potatoes)
By Chef Bruce Horowitz www.thesunkitchen.com/
Serves 6 to 8

Ingredients:

2-cup parsnip, washed and cubed
½-cup pine nuts
1½-cup water
1/3-cup lemon juice
2 clove garlic, minced - or more to taste
1 teaspoon sea salt, or to taste
1 teaspoon olive oil

Directions:

Blend all ingredients until creamy.

Serve with a drizzle of flax oil or simple gravy (½ cup chickpea miso and ½ cup water whisked with a bit of cumin, pepper or chopped mushrooms).

Vegetarian Recipes

The following recipes were provided by PETA: People for the Ethical Treatment of Animals and their vegetarian starter kit. Get yours at goveg.com!

Blueberry Pancakes

Makes 4-6 servings

Ingredients

1-cup whole-wheat flour
1-cup white flour
3-Tbsp baking powder
1-tsp sea salt
2-cups vanilla soy milk
3-Tbsp canola or safflower oil
½-cup frozen blueberries
½-cup fresh blueberries

Directions

Combine the dry ingredients in a bowl and sift together. Add the soy milk and the oil and mix until smooth.

Ladle onto a hot pancake griddle (or skillet). Add the frozen blueberries. Cook for 2-3 minutes on each side. (Flip when little bubbles start appearing in the batter.)

Serve with the fresh blueberries on top.

Crunchy Vegetable Wraps
Makes 4 servings

Ingredients
¼ cup nondairy cream cheese (try Tofutti brand)

4 10-inch flour tortillas

1 cup shredded spinach

¼ cup alfalfa sprouts

½ cup shredded red cabbage

½ cup sliced avocado

¼ cup chopped tomatoes

½ cup diced cucumbers

2 Tbsp. finely diced red onion

salt and pepper, to taste

Directions
Spread 1 Tbsp. of the "cream cheese" on each tortilla. Sprinkle an even amount of the remaining ingredients on each tortilla and roll up.

Pesto Pasta
Makes 4 servings

Ingredients
   2/3 cup basil pesto
   1 9-oz pkg. fresh fettuccine (or dry)
   1 Tbsp. olive oil
   3 cloves garlic, minced
   2 cups sliced roasted red bell peppers
   ½ cup pitted olives, halved lengthwise
    salt and pepper, to taste.

Directions
Place the pesto in a large bowl.

Cook the pasta according to the package instructions.

While the pasta is cooking, heat the oil in a large skillet over medium-high heat. Add the garlic and cook, stirring until soft and fragrant, about 30 seconds. Add the peppers and olives and cook, stirring until hot, about 3 minutes. Season with salt and pepper.

Drain the cooked pasta, reserving about 1/3 cup of the water. Whisk the pasta water into the pesto.

Add the pasta to the pesto mix and toss to combine. Serve immediately. Goes great with a toasted baguette covered in melted mozzarella cheese.

Spinach Lasagna

Makes 6-8 servings

Ingredients

½ lb. lasagna noodles

2 10-oz pkgs. Frozen chopped spinach, thawed and drained

1 lb soft tofu

1 lb firm tofu

1 Tbsp. sugar

¼ cup soymilk

½ tsp. garlic powder (or mince some fresh garlic, to taste)

2 Tbsp. lemon juice

3 tsp. minced fresh basil

2 tsp. salt

4 cups tomato sauce

Directions

Cook the lasagna noodles according to the package directions. Drain and set aside. Preheat the oven to 350°F.

Squeeze the spinach as dry as possible and set aside.

Place the tofu, sugar, soymilk, garlic powder, lemon juice, basil and salt in a food processor or blender, and blend until smooth. Stir in the spinach.

Cover the bottom of a 9 x 13-inch baking dish with a thin layer of the tomato sauce, then a layer of noodles (using about one-third of the noodles). Follow with half of the tofu filling. Continue in the same order, using half of the remaining tomato sauce and noodles and the entire remaining tofu filling. End with the remaining noodles, covered by the remaining tomato sauce.

Bake for 25-30 minutes.

Hearty "Beef" Cassoulet

Makes 4 Servings

Ingredients

6 garlic cloves, minced
1 ½-cups chopped onions
1-Tbsp dried thyme
3 bay leaves
½-tsp marjoram
1-tsp dried rosemary
3-Tbsp olive oil
½-cup red wine
1-cup pealed and sliced carrots
¾-cup sliced celery
1-cup cubed potatoes
1-cup diced tomatoes
¾-cup cubed seitan
2-Tbsp molasses
2-Tbsp Dijon mustard
1 15-oz can kidney beans, drained
1 15-oz can navy beans, drained
Sea salt and black pepper, to taste
1-cup whole wheat bread crumbs mixed with 3-Tbsp olive oil

Directions

Preheat oven to 350°F
In a large pot, sauté the garlic, onions, thyme, bay leaves, marjoram, and
    rosemary in the olive oil for about 2 minutes.
Add the wine, cover, and simmer for 5 minutes
Add the carrots, celery, potatoes, and tomatoes and simmer for 10
    minutes.
Add the seitan, molasses, mustard, beans, salt and pepper. Heat through.
Transfer to 6 15-oz oiled casserole dishes. Top with bread crumbs,
    cover, and bake for about 45 minutes.

Strawberry-Mango Crisp
Makes 6 servings

Ingredients
For the fruit mixture:
1 qt. quartered strawberries
2 cups diced mango
¼ cup sugar
¼ cup flour

For the topping:
1 cup flour
½ cup rolled oats
1 cup brown sugar
½ cup (1 stick) margarine

Directions
Preheat oven to 400°F,
Mix the ingredients for the fruit mixture together in a large bowl. Spread evenly into a 2-quart casserole dish. Set aside

Mix the dry ingredients for the topping together in a medium bowl. Cut in the margarine until the mixture resembles small peas. Spread evenly over the fruit mixture.

Bake for 35-45 minutes, or until bubbly.

Serve warm with nondairy ice cream.

An Eco-Babe Tip:

Sweet Potato Leaves (As Greens)

This recipe is made to taste not made of set amounts. So sample often and add more ingredients as needed.

Ingredients:

sweet potato leaves (they cook down like other greens so you will need to pick plenty)
minced garlic
salt (optional)

Wash leaves and stems well, the vine is not suitable for cooking as it is woody in texture.

Put water in a large pot and bring to a boil. Place leaves in boiling water add minced garlic. I used 2 tablespoons to an 8 qt pot. Boil until cooked down. Serve and enjoy!

Note: The water will be slightly slimy but not as slimy as boiled okra. Sweet Potato Leaves are surprisingly good! The first time I served them I waited until after my husband was finished to tell him what they were. He laughed and laughed and said well that is one way to get more out of our garden and to save more money.

I do not add salt due to sodium. However, my husband and son did add salt to their plates. My son kept saying "yummy greens"!
-Linda Rushing, Sales Rep. Smyrna, TN

Homemade Ice Cream

6-cups goat's milk
2-Tablespoons of vanilla
1/2-Cup organic raw agave nectar (low glycemic sweetener)

Put about 3 cups of the milk into your blender. Add vanilla and agave nectar and blend well, to thoroughly dissolve the agave nectar. Pour into ice cream freezer, add the rest of the goat's milk and freeze as you normally would.

Enjoy!
Note: Agave nectar is a wonderful natural sweetener, where a recipe calls for 1 cup of sugar you would only need 1/2 cup of Agave Nectar. And it is yummy! I find it at the local Health Food Store, Target and Publix. **-Linda Rushing, Sales Rep. Smyrna, TN**

What Are You Wearing?

The clothes we wear not only say a lot about our fashion sense and personality, but also say quite a bit about our buying habits. Do you prefer name brands or the cheapest you can find? Do you put a lot of thought into your clothes, or are they just a way to not be naked? Considering that you have purchased this book, you're probably trying to make more conscious and educated decisions about the products you buy and the way you do things. Why should clothes shopping be any different? Depending on where you shop and what you buy, you could be contributing not only to the pollution of the earth, but also to the exploitation of women and minorities.

Sweatshops

What is a sweatshop?

A sweatshop is any workplace where workers are treated unfairly and illegally in ways such as: extreme exploitation, child labor, long work hours, low wage, unsafe working conditions, verbal, sexual and/or physical abuse, and intimidation or fear tactics by management. Sweatshops can be found in roughly 200 countries with tens of thousands of factories employing tens of millions of workers. Large corporations seek out countries where they can pay the least for labor without having to deal with human rights. Sweatshops can even be found right here in the United States. The U.S. Department of Labor estimates that 67% of Los Angeles clothing factories pay less than minimum wage and fail to pay overtime[27].

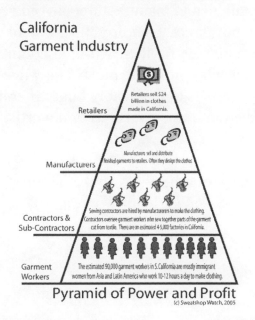

California Garment Industry

Retailers — Retailers sell $24 billion in clothes made in California.

Manufacturers — Manufacturers sell and distribute finished garments to retailers. Often they design the clothes.

Contractors & Sub-Contractors — Sewing contractors are hired by manufacturers to make the clothing. Contractors oversee garment workers who sew together parts of the garment cut from textile. There are an estimated 4-5,000 factories in California.

Garment Workers — The estimated 90,000 garment workers in S. California are mostly immigrant women from Asia and Latin America who work 10-12 hours a day to make clothing.

Pyramid of Power and Profit
(c) Sweatshop Watch, 2005

99

Why do sweatshops exist?

Sweatshops exist when corporations often have little or no accountability. The clothing industry is a hierarchy where retailers (Wal-Mart, Target, etc.) subcontract labor. The pyramid here represents the California garment industry, but it is representative of the garment industry worldwide. Because these corporations are not directly responsible for the manufacturing of the product, they have no responsibility for the employees who actually make the product. For example, retailers order from manufacturers, who design the product and then the manufactures then hire contractors to manage production. Finally, the contractors hire garment workers who actually cut, sew and assemble the product. So there are several agencies between the corporation and the garment workers[28].

There is intense competition among contractors, who have to put in the lowest bid possible to win contracts from manufacturers. These prices are driven to the point where contractors cannot afford to give garment workers a livable wage. To make a profit, they have to get as much labor as possible out of workers and "trim the fat" wherever they can. This leads to unsafe working conditions, exploitation and abuse. Again, retailers and manufacturers avoid accountability by claiming that they do not directly employ the garment workers and are therefore not responsible for their working conditions and wages. Yet, they are the ones who profit the most. The wage gap between CEOs and garment workers is unforgivably huge. If companies were willing to cut out a fraction of their salaries or advertising budgets, garment workers could have a livable wage.

Check out the chart on the next page that shows the disparity between CEOS and garment workers.

Salaries for clothing executives in 2002

CEO	Company	Annual Salary[29]	Hourly Wage[30]
Philip Marineau	Levi-Strauss & Co	$24.9 million	$11,971
Tommy Hilfiger	Tommy Hilfiger Corp	$22.4 million	$10,769
Ralph Lauren	Polo Ralph Lauren	$4.5 million	$2,163
Paul Charron	Liz Claiborne Inc.	$3.12 million	$1,500
Paul Fireman	Reebok	$3.1 million	$1,490
Philip Knight	Nike	$2.73 million	$1,312

Average hourly wage for garment workers

Country/Region	Hourly Wage[31]
Mexico	$1.75
South Africa	$1.57
Malaysia	$1.36
El Salvador	$1.08
Mauritius	$0.94
China	$0.86
India	$0.71
Sri Lanka	$0.57
Indonesia	$0.24
Pakistan	$0.23

In the garment industry profit is more important than human rights. It is part of the global economy, ruled by the free trade system. Free trade sounds like a wonderful thing, but, in reality, it is anything but. The NAFTA (North American Free Trade Agreement) and GATT (General Agreement of Tariffs and Trade) opened the door for large corporations to export jobs to developing countries and save money on labor costs. The developing countries are promised market access by removing trade barriers like taxes and tariffs. Prior to the free trade system, outside countries would have to pay for the privilege of exporting their goods into the U.S. The problem with this system is that it does not include strong social provisions for the treatment of employees or the environment.

The article "The Globetrotting Sneaker" by Cynthia Enloe[32] (published in MS. Magazine in 1995) illustrates what happened in the 1980s when major U.S. shoe manufactures Nike and Reebok closed down factories in the United States and subcontracted labor to foreign-owned companies in South Korea and Taiwan. The United States lost over 58,000 jobs. The South Korean and Taiwanese governments were happy to accept our jobs because it gave them a way to suppress labor organizing and reinforce the subordination of their women. "With their sense of patriotic duty, Korean women seemed the ideal labor force for export-oriented factories" (Enloe). At least seventy-six percent of all garment workers are women. The men are usually in a position of power over the women. The trend by U.S. corporations to outsource labor leads to inequality among the male and female workers in these foreign countries and the United States.

The fact that U.S. corporations do not want to have to "deal" with the health and safety of women workers shows that, to them, women are nothing more than chattel. It is additionally disturbing because the Confucian philosophy of South Korea and Taiwan "measured a [woman's] morality by her willingness to work hard for her family's well-being and to acquiesce to her father's and husband's dictates" (Enloe). This meant that no matter how difficult things were for the women, they would continue to work, as compelled by their religion, fathers, and husbands.

What these foreign-owned companies did not foresee was the uprising of their women workers. While the U.S. giants turned their backs, the foreign government stepped in to break up the employee uprising. "Troops sexually assaulted women workers, stripping, fondling, and raping them 'as a control mechanism for suppressing women's engagement in the labor movement" (Enloe). They did this because they feared the movement would shake the foundations of the entire political system. Despite this, activists stood up and started the Korean Women Workers Association. They fought for shorter hours, better pay, health care and the ending of sexual assault. By 1990, women earned more than 50% of male wages (about $2 an hour). This made a big difference, and may have been a catalyst for ending the military regime and forcing open elections in 1987.

Seeing an end to their enslavement of workers and big profits, Nike uprooted and moved onto China, Indonesia, and Thailand. All of these countries were controlled by authoritarian regimes that wanted women kept hard at work with low pay ($.10 an hour) and no way to organize. This caused lost jobs in South Korea and Taiwan and forced many women into sex work. Of all occupations in the world, sex work takes advantage of women in the worst ways. It is not only demeaning work that separates women from their own pleasure, but it is not a field in which women can progress or improve their situation. Sex work is one of those fields, especially when one is in the lowest economic strata where those so employed may never rise above their poverty. It perpetuates that which is keeping the women from improving their lives. This is especially distressing in Korea, because their Confucian philosophy would leave the women feeling forced to continue their sex work in order to fulfill the requirements of their religion.

Not only do foreign women suffer, but American women suffer as well. Prior to manufacturing and textile companies leaving the United States, they primarily employed non-Caucasian women. This means that hundreds of thousands, possibly millions of American women have been laid-off or fired because of exported jobs. This has been a catalyst for women's poverty in the United States. Women are trying to create links among these countries to make it harder to keep female wages so low. They are trying to change the politics of consumerism, rather than consumerism itself. The reality of free trade is that of high profits and slavery that is no different than that of the U.S. slave trade in the 1700s[33].

To summarize the free trade system:

- U.S. consumers demand cheaper clothes.
- Women in the U.S. lose jobs when their factories are exported to developing countries so contractors can pay less for labor.
- This leads to increased poverty among U.S. women and increased strain on social welfare programs.
- Because of the competition in the global economy, wages and working conditions are driven down.
- Foreign garment workers are exploited and abused by their employers who are seeking to "sweat" profits out of them.
- When foreign workers demand their rights and try to form unions, manufacturers fire/abuse them or move on to other countries to avoid giving in to their demands.
- When workers in the U.S. demand their rights, employers threaten to report undocumented workers and have them deported.
- When manufactures leave one foreign country for another, many of the women left behind are forced into sex work.
- Meanwhile retailers and manufactures enjoy higher profits.
- Consumers continue purchasing clothes from sweatshops, which reinforces the entire system.

Are there laws to protect workers?

Yes and no. There are some laws in the United States (such as the Fair Labor Standards Act and the minimum wage), but they are often poorly enforced. Sometimes it takes months, even years for cases to be resolved due to the amount of complaints and the lack of government officials to see to them. Immigrant workers may be afraid to report abuse because they fear deportation. In addition, those with limited English skills may not know of the laws or understand our bureaucratic system. Internationally, the labor standards created by the International Labor Organization cannot be legally enforced. To attract American companies and money, some foreign nations will weaken their labor and environmental laws. Additionally, managers who are hungry for profit will often do a poor job of monitoring labor standards, instead pushing employees as hard as they can to get every bit of labor out of them possible.

Why do companies use child labor, and don't these jobs help the child's family survive?

There are several reasons why companies use child labor. The common excuse is that the children are less likely to complain about bad working conditions than adults. Child labor is actually a symptom of a larger social problem of consumerism and the widening gap between the classes. It happens when adult workers do not have a living wage and/or live in poverty stricken neighborhoods. If they can't afford childcare and have no schools to send their children to, parents often have little choice but to bring their children to work. A major problem with child labor is that the children are often subjected to working conditions even worse than those of the parents. They are treated as less than human with long hours, dangerous working conditions, lack of proper food and medical care, and slave-like conditions. Some children are even sold into child labor when the family can no longer afford to care for them.

What can I do?

Believe it or not, you can do a lot just by altering whom you buy your clothes from. Consumers exert a massive amount of influence on retailers. If retailers see a drop in profits, they will have to reform their practices. However, it may take a bit of sleuthing to find sweatshop-free clothes and I will do everything I can to make this easy for you! As I stated before, there are tens of thousands of garment factories around the world, so it's difficult to narrow down just who is doing what. The Disney Corporation alone has over 20,000 factories. Retailers do not have to disclose the locations of their factories, but there are clues that you can look for, for sweatshop free clothes.

- Unions

Clothes made from factories with democratic unions will have a union label. Workers in unions have achieved or are striving for a living wage, safe working conditions, and fair treatment. Unions allow employees to bargain with employers without fear of retaliation.

- Worker-Owned Cooperatives

Otherwise known as co-ops, worker-owned cooperatives are businesses that are collectively owned and operated by the workers. This means that the workers share the profits.

- Fair Trade Organizations

These are entities that work with small businesses, cooperatives and communities to ensure that they are treated fairly. These organizations band workers together to help them start businesses, reduce costs for supplies, and receive higher and otherwise fair prices for their goods. Workers are paid better and profits are reinvested into the business and community. Because of fair trade organizations, communities work toward sustainability and can afford health facilities and schools. In addition, workers are trained in literacy, leadership, and business skills.

If you want to look up specific companies to see their labor practices, there are

An Eco-Babe's Tip: We live in a consumerist society and we are often pressured to buy things we don't need. So I fight back by asking myself, "Is this a need or a not?" Not only does this save me a lot of money, but it also saves me from feeling guilty when the credit card bill comes in. After doing this for a while, you will notice that you don't have a lot of junk around the house, you take less trips to drop stuff off at goodwill and you have saved enough money to buy yourself something really cool, like those fancy boots you've been drooling over for months
– Elizabeth Estrella, Personal Banker, Prescott Valley, AZ.

several online resources to help you. Please see the "Resources" at the end of this chapter. Check out the Internet Shopping Guide in the appendices for a sampling of union and fair trade clothing brands.

Deadly Cotton

Just as non-organic beauty products are harmful for our health and environment, so are non-organic garments. Cotton is grown on 2.4% of the world's land suitable for crops; two-thirds of which is grown in developing countries. It's a $30 billion a year industry and is responsible for the release of over $2 billion worth of pesticides every year; half of which are classified as hazardous to our health[34]. The problems with cotton, otherwise known as "white gold," are a giant elephant in the room that no one wants to talk about.

Pesticides and Cotton

Pesticides are chemicals made specifically to kill. Sometimes, they are designed to kill bugs or unwanted plants; other times, bacteria, mold and/or fungi. Unfortunately, pesticides are very good at their job and affect not only the pests, but also the animals that feed on the pests, and even humans. Cotton is the most polluting and the most polluted crop in the world. Insecticides account for 60% of the chemicals used on cotton, which is 16% of the total amount of insecticide used in the world. No other crop comes close.

The World Health Organization estimates that 25 to 77 million agricultural workers get pesticide poisoning each year and 20,000 of those die. There are no specific figures for how many of those poisonings are due to cotton production, but half of all pesticides used in developing countries are used on cotton.

> Acute symptoms of pesticide poisoning include headaches, vomiting, tremors, lack of coordination, difficulty breathing or respiratory depression, loss of consciousness, seizures and death. Chronic effects of long-term pesticide exposure include impaired

memory and concentration, disorientation, severe depression and confusion[35].

The vast majority of pesticide poisonings and 99% of related deaths occur in developing nations. Children are especially vulnerable to poisoning, which puts child laborers and children living near cotton farms at risk. Pesticides are also hazardous to the environment. Runoff from cotton farms seeps into the groundwater and contaminates rivers and lakes. This puts anyone who drinks and bathes in that water at risk. In addition, animals that eat the poisoned plants and insects can also be poisoned and die, which throws the ecosystem off balance.

Water and Cotton

Cotton requires a lot of water. It is known as the world's thirstiest crop. It takes over 96 oz of water to grow a single cotton bud and 528 gallons to make a single cotton shirt. Because most of cotton is grown in developing countries and exported, it is they who suffer from the amount of water consumed. Unfortunately these cotton-producing countries include places like India and Uzbekistan, which need clean water the most. As mentioned before, pesticides poison groundwater, but that is not the only trouble caused by runoff. The high impact of irrigation, dam construction and drainage, to name a few, causes salinization, loss of soil, and loss of biodiversity.

The Aral Sea in Uzbekistan is an example of just such effects. It was once the world's fourth largest inland body of water. After it was tapped for irrigation, it shrunk to just 15% of its former volume. It is almost 600% more saline (amount of salt in the water) and none of the native fish remain. So much of the former seabed is now exposed that you could fit six million soccer pitches inside it! This has ended the commercial fishing industry in the area, which used to harvest 40,000 tons of fish, and stripped away many food sources (water fowl, fish, plants, large game)[36]. Pesticides are also quickly diminishing the Great Barrier Reef off the coast of Australia. You can read more about it here:

108

http://www.theaustralian.news.com.au/story/0,20867,21268303-
5006786,00.html.

Here are a few of the common pesticides used in cotton, provided by the Environmental Justice Foundation.

Aldicarb, a powerful nerve agent, is one of the most toxic pesticides applied to cotton worldwide and the 2nd most commonly used pesticide in global cotton production. Just one drop of aldicarb, absorbed through the skin, is enough to kill an adult.

Endosulfan, is widely used in cotton production and is the dominant pesticide in the cotton sector in 19 countries. In a single province of Benin, at least 37 people died from endosulfan poisoning in just one cotton season.

Monocrotophos, despite being withdrawn from the US market in 1989, it is widely used in developing world countries. In 1997, Paraguay's Ministry of Health and Welfare identified it as being responsible for causing paralysis in children living in cotton growing areas.

Deltamethrin, a nerve agent is applied in over half of the cotton producing countries. Medical analysis in a community in a South African village located on the edge of a major cotton production area found traces of deltamethrin in human breast milk.

Resources

So now that you have an understanding of the problems associated with sweatshops and cotton production, as well as a grasp of shopping organically, it's time to put all that together. Our goal as contentious and educated babes is to purchase clothes that are made ethically and from organic ingredients. Lucky for us, many fair trade items are also organic. For brands and businesses that sell fair trade and organic products, please visit the *Internet Shopping Guide* in the Appendix. For more information about fair trade and organic clothing, please check out the following resources.

Corp Watch - Information on labor, environmental and shareholder actions, and how to request data through the Freedom of Information Act. (Corpwatch.org)

Responsible Shopper Search Engine (Responsibleshopper.org)

Transnationale - Find out the parent companies of a brand and their human rights records. (Transnationale.org)

Sweatshop Watch (Sweatshopwatch.org)

California Department of Labor (Dir.ca.gov)

Federal OSHA (Osha.gov)

Fair Trade Federation (Fairtradefederation.com)

Environmental Justice Foundation (Ejfoundation.org)

World Health Organization (Who.int)

An Eco-Babe Business:
PM Organics - Textiles You Feel Good About!
http://www.pmorganics.com

I am a work-at-home mom who started this business when my daughter was a little over 3 years old and I realized that there was very little organic fabric and clothing available. Since then, the industry has exploded and you can find organic clothes even at Wal-Mart. However, I focus on finding beautiful organic fabrics with an emphasis on US-made as much as possible. For people who cannot afford to buy organic clothing ready-made, making it yourself is the perfect solution. And for people who already sew and want to switch to organic items, I am there to provide those beautiful fabrics. - **Marie DiCocco, Middlesex, VT**

Babes at Home

Detoxing Your Home

Our homes are our sanctuaries. The place we turn to, to heal, relax, refuel, and grow. They are also one of the most toxic environments we come in contact with! By detoxing your home, you may find relief from common ailments caused from mold, mildew, dust, and other hidden toxins. Let's take a closer look at your home and address some of the common problems and remedies.

Quick tips for total home care:

- Use compact florescent bulbs (CFLs) throughout your house. By switching just 5 regular light bulbs to CFLs, you could save $60 a year! (LEDs are even better, but are still fairly expensive.) Do not throw away CFLs as they must be recycled properly. They contain mercury, which is toxic. Contact your local waste management company to find out where and how.
- If you insist of using regular light bulbs, install dimmers to save electricity and only use as much lighting as you need.
- Use solar lighting in your landscape.
- Use a solar charger to charge your phone, iPod, and laptop.
- Unplug chargers and appliances when you are not using them.
- Use power strips to make turning off unused electronics easier. Even when electronics like your TV, stereo, and DVD player are turned off, they still use energy because of their standby mode. Together, it's like having a 100 watt light bulb on constantly! So plug them into a power strip and then turn that strip off when they are not in use.
- Set your computer to "sleep" or "hibernate" when you step away from it. Further, make sure you shut down at the end of the day and turn off the power strip. You can find the power management settings in the control panel if you run Windows or system preferences if you run a Mac.
- Sweep, rather than spray down your driveway and sidewalk.
- Landscape with native plants because they won't require excessive watering.

- Use a rain barrel to collect water from your roof's downspout to irrigate your garden.
- Buy blackout curtains if you can't afford double or triple-pane windows. This will reduce heat loss in the winter; and if you live in the desert, blocking out the sun will help keep the house cooler.
- Caulk around your outlets, switches and windows, and put insulating foam gaskets behind your outlets and switches. This will help keep good weather in and bad weather out.
- Make sure all exposed pipes are well insulated.
- Hot air rises, so make sure your attic is properly insulated and ventilated.
- Sign up for electronic billing, to limit the amount of mail you receive and therefore save trees.
- Read your favorite newspapers and magazines online, as opposed to getting printed copies.
- If you are remodeling your home, shop for new fixtures and construction supplies from Habitat for Humanity shops. (www.habitat.org/env/restores.aspx). There you can find everything from light fixtures, to toilets, and doors!
- Cut the junk mail! We waste over 100 million trees to make junk mail. Stop the insanity! Check out the following websites for: www.greendimes.com, and www.junkbusters.com, You can also contact the distributors of all of the junk mail and catalogs you receive and ask them to take you off their mailing list.
- Have as many green plants in your house as possible. They cleanse the air and look great.

An Eco-Babe's Tip: Shop in bulk whenever you can to save money and cut packaging waste. Think about your purchases in not only how they are made and who made them, but also in how they are disposed. – **Summer Henry, Tattoo Artist and Teacher, Prescott Valley, AZ.**

Room by Room: The Bathroom

Cleaning Products

Most bathroom cleaners contain harsh chemicals and toxins to get that perfect shine, but they can damage your skin and respiratory system, as well as the environment. Thankfully, companies are beginning to take notice and develop products that not only leave your bathroom squeaky clean, but also are safe for you and the planet. So, where to start? I suggest you start by gradually replacing your cleaners with more eco-friendly versions as you finish your current supply.

In this case, you don't need to read the labels, because household products are very straightforward. When it comes to conventional household cleaners, all of them are toxic in some form. What makes them so dangerous is the fact that they contain synthetic chemicals that can damage your eyes and skin if you come in contact with them, and that those chemicals give off fumes that can damage your respiratory system. These fumes are called Volatile Organic Compounds (VOCs) and in this case, the term organic doesn't mean natural, as in healthy, but natural as in something that exists in this world. Chlorine Bleach is one such product. It is not only a poisonous gas, but a neurotoxin and carcinogenic. So unless you are a hundred percent sure that your current products are nontoxic, every product you currently have needs to be replaced with an eco-friendly version.

Here are the some of the major chemicals you want to avoid: chlorine bleach, phosphates, glycol ether (2-butoxyethanol, has a strong pine or citrus smell), and alkylphenol ethoxylates (APEs). Be wary of fake organic products. Meaning just because they say they are nontoxic, hypoallergenic, phosphate free, biodegradable or natural, doesn't mean that they are worthy.

My favorite brands are Mrs. Meyer's, Ecover's and Seventh Generation (I just love the minty-freshness of their toilet cleaner!). You will want to purchase cleaners that list all of their ingredients on the label, are biodegradable, and that do not contain any toxic chemicals. For example, here are the ingredients to Seventh Generations Toilet Bowl Cleaner: *Aqua (water), lactic acid (plant-derived demineralizer), polyglucose, coceth-7, coceth-4 and deceth-5 (plant-derived cleaning agents), xanthan gum (natural thickener), essential oils and botanical extracts* (citrus aurantifolia (lime), abies balsamea (balsam fir), calilistris columellaris (emerald cypress). *d-limonene is a naturally occurring component of these ingredients*[37]. If you're a stickler for brands and want to stick with one you know and trust, try Clorox's Green Works line, which includes all-purpose, glass, bathroom, and toilet-bowl cleaners. And speaking of toilets, don't use toilet deodorizers or "toilet cakes" as those just pour bad chemicals down the toilet.

You can also make your own cleaning products with common household ingredients. For example, lemon juice can get rid of mineral stains. Just spray the surface of your sink or tub, let it sit for about a half hour and scrub. Lime scale clogging your showerhead or faucet? Just soak it in white vinegar for an hour. Then rinse and reattach.

Water

There are many ways to conserve water in the bathroom. You can reduce water consumption significantly by installing low-flow aerators on your faucets and showerheads. They work by mixing air into the water so you use less water to get the same amount of pressure. Low-flow aerators are inexpensive and can be installed in minutes. You just screw them into place.

Showerheads

Bricor (www.bricor.com) makes a one-gallon-per-minute showerhead that is best for those who like strong pressure because the water practically explodes with aerated power. Gaiam (www.gaiam.com) makes a 1.2-gallon per minute (the Lowest Flow) showerhead that is equipped with a "soap-up valve," which lets you pause the water flow while you get sudsy or shave. For those on a budget, Home Depot sells Flowise, a 1.5-gallon per minute showerhead for $20-70. To save water for free, just turn off the tap while brushing your teeth and fill the basin for washing or shaving.

Toilets

You can take water consumption another step forward by installing dual-flush toilet tanks. They have two flushing options, which use more or less water depending on how much/what you are flushing. You can even retrofit your existing toilet with this option. Check out Caroma, Aquanotion (www.dualflushtoilet.net), and TwoFlush. Another option is to have your toilet reuse grey water from the sink or you can go a step further and try Envirolet, which uses NO water by composting waste instead.

If your toilet was installed before 1992, it's probably a water hog. You will need to add a toilet dam to reduce the amount of water flowing out of it. Toilet dams make your tank smaller with plastic barriers that limit the amount of water used. If possible, replace your old toilet with a one of the previous water friendly options. In my house, we also follow, "If it's yellow, let it mellow. If it's brown, flush it down." This saves several gallons of water a day.

Water Heaters

Hot water accounts for 13 percent of the average household's annual electricity bill, or about $247[38]. Save electricity by installing a solar hot water heater! Your electric company may even give you a rebate for doing so. They are not as hard to find as you think; Home Depot sells solar hot water heaters in most cities. Another option is a tank-less hot water-on-demand system. With this you don't have to waste money and electricity by storing and maintaining hot water like you do with a conventional water heater. The hot water-on-demand systems are units that attach directly to the water outlet (faucets-under the sink, bath-in the wall). They do not store water; rather they heat it as it flows through the pipes, a moment before it comes out of the faucet or bath. You only heat, what you use. They cost around $300-700.

If you don't have the money to buy a new hot water system, make sure you insulate your tank. This keeps the heat from radiating away from the tank and makes it so your heater doesn't have to work as hard to keep the water hot. You can also set the thermostat on your water heater between 120 and 130 degrees. Lower temperatures may save energy, but you might run out of hot water or your heater will have to work harder to make your water hotter for the dishwasher or washing machine.

Mold

Mold grows in dark and wet areas and can quickly become a problem. Not only does mold cause structural damage, but it can also damage your lungs. Mold is linked to allergies, asthma and other health problems. So it is imperative that you stop this problem at its source by checking all your pipes and fixing any leaks. Use tea tree oil to kill any growths of mold that you find. Wear gloves, and a mask when cleaning mold. If the growth is big you should hire a professional.

Towels and Paper

The traditional process of growing cotton and bleaching paper pulp contributes *billions of billions* of pounds of fertilizer and pesticides to our planet each year. You can do your part to reduce that number by using organic bath towels and recycled or organic toilet paper. You can even try bamboo, kenaf, and hemp products. Bamboo products are very soft and require no pesticides or fertilizer to grow. Also use a PVC-free shower curtain and bath mat. PVC means polyvinyl chloride, which is a toxic plastic. It is linked to reproductive problems, birth defects and liver tumors in mice. You can find those at IKEA, or try hemp, as it's naturally antibacterial and resistant to mold. You can find great cork bath mats at www.realgoods.com. They are naturally antifungal, which is great if you have an athlete in your house.

Conventional toilet paper is subject to the same bleaching process as menstrual products; see "The Moon Wise Visitor" chapter. Therefore, toilet paper and all other bleached paper products contain dioxin. Use recycled and unbleached paper products. The Natural Resources

Defense Council created a great guide at:
http://www.nrdc.org/land/forests/gtissue.asp
It will help you choose the best paper products for your home. I personally chose to use Seventh Generation paper products.

Room by Room: The Kitchen

Eating Organic

Choosing organic foods is the best way to eliminate dangerous pesticides from your diet. Please read the chapter "The Yummy Tummy" for more information about purchasing organic foods. Remember to rinse your vegetables and fruits and if necessary, peel them to remove the chemicals. Again, organic produce is best, because peeling removes a very large portion of the nutrients. It's also important to wash foods such as cantaloupe and watermelon, because when you cut them, you could pass bacteria and pesticides from the rind into the meat of the fruit, with the knife.

> Use old t-shirts, socks and boxer shorts to dust and clean house. No one needs to know! Keep a bin of these rags in your kitchen and bath and use them to clean up instead of towels.
>
> You can also try using cloth handkerchiefs instead of tissues.

Water and Power

Just like the bathroom, you can save water by installing faucet aerators. You can even go another step further and install a low water dishwasher. Make sure you wash your fruits and vegetables in a bowl, and fill your sink to wash and rinse dishes, instead of running the water. When you wash dishes in the dishwasher, wash only full loads and set the dishwasher to the shortest cycle necessary. Not everything needs to be washed on the heaviest setting. I like to turn on the dishwasher on my way out the door in the morning, so I put it on the air dry setting. It takes a little longer, but since I'm not home, it doesn't matter. The air dry setting uses up less energy than heat dry.

By adjusting the temperature on your refrigerator and freezer, you can save money. Make sure your refrigerator temperature is set somewhere between 38 to 42 degrees Fahrenheit. Your freezer should be set between 0 and 5 degrees Fahrenheit. If your refrigerator has one, take advantage of the power-save switch. Just check your fridge's user guide to find out if you have one. If you lost your user guide, most manufacturers post them on the internet. You can make sure your fridge's door seals tightly by closing the door over a dollar bill. If that dollar bill slides easily with the door closed, then you need to replace the door gaskets.

Tap Water

Repeat after me: Bottled water is not healthier than tap water. In some cases, it can be worse than your tap water because it is not highly regulated. Bottled water is held only to the standards of the Food and Drug Administration, whereas tap water is held to the higher standards of the Environmental Protection Agency. If you are nervous, have your tap water tested and/or install a water filter. Water purifiers vary from $10 carafes, to several hundred-dollar water softening systems. I find a filter that attaches onto the tap, to be the easiest to maintain.

Cookware

Perfluorochemicals, which are synthetic heat-resisting chemicals that are linked to several health problems, are found in non-stick cookware. The danger is found in scratched up pots and pans, the scratches allowing the chemicals to reach us. A better option is to use old-fashioned cast-iron cookware. It is durable, safe, and has been used for generations without ill effect. Used properly, it is naturally non-stick, and is even oven safe. Cast iron, however, works best on gas stoves. You can also try stainless –steel pans, or GreenPan, which sells non-stick pots and pans without the dangerous chemicals.

Soap

Antibacterial soaps may be causing more harm than they're worth because they allow bacterial to build up a resistance to them. Bacteria are mutating and becoming stronger. In addition, antibacterial soaps do not protect us from viruses, such as the cold or flu, which is why we are sick most of the time. Unless you have a poor immune system or have infants in the house, regular soap will work just fine. However, you can use a natural bacterial killing agent if you must. A few drops of tea tree oil mixed with water and sprayed on your countertops and children's toys, will kill off bacteria. Avoid anti-bacterial air fresheners, as they just add more chemicals into our already dirty indoor air.

Baggin' It

How many bags do you use and throw away in a given week? How about other containers like water bottles? Here are a few facts[39] to think about:

- Plastic bags and other plastic garbage thrown into the ocean kill as many as 1,000,000 sea creatures every year!
- Americans throw away 25,000,000 plastic beverage bottles every hour!
- Recycling plastic saves twice as much energy as burning it in an incinerator.
- Americans throw away 25,000,000,000 Styrofoam coffee cups every year.
- Plastic bags can take over 400 years to break down.
- Every month, we throw out enough glass bottles and jars to fill up a giant skyscraper. All of these jars are recyclable!
- The energy saved from recycling one glass bottle can run a 100-watt light bulb for four hours. It also causes 20% less air pollution and 50% less water pollution than when a new bottle is made from raw materials.
- A modern glass bottle would take 4000 years or more to decompose -- and even longer if it's in the landfill.
- If you had a 15-year-old tree and made it into paper grocery bags, you'd get about 700 of them. A supermarket could use all of

them in under an hour! This means in one year, one supermarket goes through 60,500,000 paper bags! Imagine how many supermarkets there are in the U.S!

Oi! Are you feeling a little guilty and overwhelmed? Do not fear there is much that you can do. Let's figure out reusable options for the types of containers/utensils we commonly throw away[40].

Water Bottles

Bottled water is not cleaner/safer than tap water. In fact, many brands of bottled water use regular city water as opposed to the magical spring water their names imply. The only difference is that the water is filtered at a private depot after it has been filtered by the city. If you have a soft water system or filter on your tap, you are essentially doing the same thing. That is why our dependency on gourmet water is redundant. Save yourself a ton of money and use a reusable water bottle. If you are concerned about the chemicals that plastic bottles (see caution) can give off, I recommend you use a stainless steel water bottle. Try Klean Kanteen (www.kleankanteen.com) or Sigg (www.mysigg.com) bottles. Prices range from $5 to $20.

Lunch Bags

Rather than using a paper or plastic bag to store your lunch in, how about getting a trendy reusable bag! My favorite is the Laptop style lunch box, which includes utensils, and reusable containers. It's an all-in-one system. You could also use a cloth bag. Lunch systems average $20.

Sandwich Bags

Enter the Wrap-n-Mat, invented by a woman, and revolutionizing lunchtime! It's a placemat and sandwich container in one. It closes with a hook and loop fastener. You can probably use it for other foods as well such as pizza, cake, and other square shaped foods. The Wrap-n-Mat is plastic on one side and cloth on the other. Even though they are reusable, don't put it in the washing machine or dishwasher. Heat + Plastic = melted mess. Hand wash with soap and water and air dry. $6.95

Snack Containers

You can use Gladware to hold your snacks, invest in an all-in-one lunch system, or make a little bag out of some sturdy fabric.
Pyrex is a great option for those avoiding plastic. Depending on your style, containers range from $2-10. Check out **nubiousorganics.com** for some cute options.

Plastic plates/bowls/utensils

Once again, all-in-one lunch systems include everything you need. If you don't want to purchase anything special, and have space at work/school you can just leave a few things from home there. I've had plenty of office jobs, and I would always use the bottom drawer of my desk as my kitchen. I kept a plate, bowl, cup, utensils, and dish soap in there. However, for the most part, the container I store my meal in, is the container I eat out of. No use in dirtying an extra plate is there!

> *An Eco-Babe's Tip:* My sister and I keep supplies of canvas and other reusable bags in our cars. We use them wherever we shop. It's a little thing we do to help the environment.
> **– Melody, Math Instructor, El Dorado, KS**

Shopping Bags

European countries are way ahead of America in respect to shopping bags.
After college, I backpacked in Ireland for a few months. The first time I went grocery shopping I was confused when the cashier asked for my bag. They have plastic bags just like we do, but they charge .05 Euro per bag used. Most people use cloth bags that they bring from home. This

system of punishing waste and rewarding conservation has been in place for many years. It looks as though this is how things are going to be in the U.S. soon so you might as well switch now.

While many grocery stores now sell reusable bags, you don't have to purchase them there. There are many websites where you can buy trendy, colorful and even custom bags. Some people are even making them themselves! Visit my website at **StephanieByng.com** for links.

I had an entire cabinet full of plastic bags from grocery stores. I keep them to line my bathroom trashcan. Eventually, I just had way too many. That is when I found out that most grocery stores recycle plastic bags. Just look for the bin near the entrance!

Caution: Studies have shown that contaminants in plastic may get into our foods. A study by Consumer Reports[41] showed that store-bought cheeses wrapped in Type 3 (PVC/Vinyl) plastic film contained high levels of a toxin linked to reproductive problems, birth defects, and liver tumors in mice. Do your homework before purchasing any plastic container. Avoid any that are made from Type 3 (PVC) or Type 7 (contains bisphenol-A [BPA]). Look on the bottom of the container for the number. If there isn't a number, don't buy it. Plastic wrap can also contain PVC. The safer choices are plastics 1, 2, 4 and 5[42]. This number can be found inside the chasing arrows recycle symbol. Play it safe for foods you will store at home and use glass. Avoid using plastic to heat up your food. Try glass or ceramic. Recycle plastic containers when they are old or scratched.

Room by Room: The Laundry Room

Cleaning Products

Extend the life of your clothes while keeping the environment and your skin safe. The best products for your laundry will be all natural, biodegradable, free of phosphates, and packaged in recycled/recyclable packaging. Even better would be products that are concentrated which allow you to do more loads with less packaging. Brands I love include Ecover, Seventh Generation (try Free & Clear if you have sensitive skin) and Cleanut. Speaking of nuts…

Are You Nuts?

No, not you! Your laundry! Meet one of the world's oldest eco-friendly inventions: Laundry Soap Nuts. Okay, it's not so much an invention because they grow on trees. The dried fruit of the Chinese Soapberry tree contains saponin, which is a natural cleaner that has been used for thousands of years to clean fabrics! They are amazingly effective and 100% safe for your skin and delicate fabrics. With these, you can get rid of your detergents and softeners.

To summarize, soap nuts are:
- 100% biodegradable
- ideal for silk and wool
- hypoallergenic
- fresh smelling
- brightens colors
- natural fabric softener
- low sudsing
- no chemicals
- sustainably harvested.
- Vegan (not an animal byproduct; don't eat it though!)

How to Use

Simply put some nuts into a cotton sack and add the sack to your washing machine. Follow the manufacturer's instructions. When they are used up (they can be used more than once), just add them to your compost or toss in the trash. They are 100% natural and therefore 100% biodegradable. Depending on the size of the load, soap nuts can be reused 2-5 times.

How many nuts?

Washing with warm/hot water – use 2 nuts in the cotton sack.

Washing with cold water – use 4 nuts and reuse them 2/3 times. OR pre-soak 2 Soap Nuts in the cotton sack in hot water for a few minutes. Add the "tea" and sack to your cold wash load.

Heavy Soils - Pre-soak 4 Soap Nuts in the cotton sack in hot water for a few minutes. Add the "tea" and sack to your wash load. Add fewer clothes to your machine so the fabric has lots of room to agitate.

For Sparkling Whites-Always separate your colors. For extra stain removal, add a scoop of oxygen bleach or baking soda.

Fabric Softener-Maggie's Soap Nuts naturally soften and add body to your clothes. You'll love how your clothes feel after washing with Soap Nuts. You can also add a ½-cup of vinegar to the rinse cycle for extra softening.

Hand Washables-Soak 2 Soap Nuts in hot water for a few minutes. Add the "tea" to your cool water basin. Alternatively, add a squirt of your homemade **Maggie's Soap Nuts liquid cleaner*** to the cool basin.

The previous was provided by the Maggie's Soap Nuts website at **maggiespureland.com.** *Maggie's is also available in a concentrated liquid form.

Whiter Whites

Bleach contains chlorine, which is a harmful respiratory irritant. Having whiter whites is nice, and you don't need irritated lungs to get it. Non-chlorine bleaches or oxygen bleaches are readily available and really work well. Try Seventh Generation, Ecover, and Biokleen. You can also make your own non-chlorine bleaching agent by using soap nuts, half-cup borax per load, lemons and boiling water or baking soda.

Water and Power

Washing machines vary widely in the amount of energy and water they use. If you are in the market for a new one, make sure you purchase one with the Energy Star label. Additionally, front-loading machines use about half the amount of water and energy as the average top-loading machine. Use cold water to wash your clothes whenever possible because, compared to hot water, cold water washing can reduce the energy used for washing clothes by as much as 60 percent.

Clothes dryers typically cost less than 90 dollars a year to run, but they emit several hundreds of pounds of carbon-dioxide emissions every year. Save your wallet and the planet by line drying. Anyone can line dry their clothes, even apartment dwellers. If you have outdoor space, all you need is some rope and 2 poles or trees.

126

An Eco-Babe Tip: I can't say enough great things about soap nuts! When we recently moved, my husband and I made an agreement that we were going to try and live as natural and green as possible. For us, this started with our choice in cleaning products. Not only did we need something that was safe to use around our kids, we also needed something that could clean up after them! Soap Nuts are a miracle of nature! We use them for laundry, general cleaning, hand soap, everything! As a cloth-diapering mom, I love how soft my diapers (and all my other laundry) feel without the use of my fabric softeners or other chemical additives (which are a big no-no for cloth diapers). Even my line-dried clothes are softer after switching to soap nuts. – **Megan Christensen, Work at Home mom of 2 and one on the way, Kingman, AZ.,**

If you don't, you can use A-framed racks or wood drying racks placed on your balcony or in your bathtub. Air-dried clothes never suffer from static cling, but they can get stiff and crunchy. To avoid that, use less detergent and add a half a cup of vinegar to your load during the wash cycle. It also helps to hang your clothes on a windy day and in a partially shaded spot. Also, hang the heavier parts of your clothes, facing downward.

If you must use a clothes dryer, ditch the dryer sheets. They contain chemicals that are suspected carcinogens. One option is to use a homemade sachet filled with herbs and essential oils instead, or you can add a half-cup of vinegar to your load during the rinse cycle. Always empty out the lint trap after every load. It helps the dryer to run efficiently and reduces the chance of a fire.

Dry Clean Only

Perchloroethylene, a chemical that has been linked to cancer and reduced fertility, is relied on my most dry cleaners to clean your garments. So if you must dry clean, seek out a business that uses silicone solvent-based or liquid CO_2 cleaning methods. Avoid places that use the following: Hydrocarbon, Solvair, and Greanearth. Or, just wash the clothes yourself. It is ok for most dry clean garments, including wool, cashmere and silk, to be gently hand-washed. Even better, don't buy synthetic clothes that require dry cleaning. Check out these websites to find a green dry cleaner: www.nodryclean.com and www.findco2.com.

Final tip, underwear and socks aside, try to wear your clothes more than once before you toss them in the hamper. Less laundry equals less water and electricity used.

Room by Room: The Living/Family Room

Air

Our homes may be our sanctuaries, but the air is often more polluted than the world outside. The Environmental Protection Agency estimates that indoor air is 2 - 5 times worse than outside! It's because the very things our homes are comprised of give off chemicals such as formaldehyde and benzene: particleboard, fiberboard, carpets with PCV backing, and varnishes and paints made of volatile organic compounds (VOCs). You don't have to completely redecorate your home, as there are some inexpensive ways you can reduce the pollution. Keep rooms well ventilated and, especially in the winter, open your windows occasionally. Take your shoes off at the door so you don't track outdoor pollutants throughout the house. Clean and/or replace the filters on your air-conditioner and furnace often. Keep your air ducts clear and regularly service your air-conditioner and furnace units.

If you are up for redecorating, remember these tips:
- Avoid wall-to-wall carpeting.
- Avoid stain resistant furniture.
- Try to buy either antique furniture or furniture made from sustainable materials and without synthetic varnishes.
- Avoid anything made of PVC/Vinyl.
- Buy linens, pillows and window dressings in either organic or sustainable materials.
- Use Low or No VOC paint.

According to the Environmental Protection Agency (EPA), Radon gas is the cause of 21,000 lung cancer deaths every year. It's a radioactive gas that can accumulate in buildings. The EPA estimates that one out of every 15 American homes has elevated levels of radon. So do yourself a favor and test your home for radon. Buy a do-it-yourself radon testing-kit from any hardware store, or hire a qualified radon tester. Also, get a fire detector that also checks for carbon monoxide, which can quickly accumulate during the winter when the heater is on. It is really important to open a window during the winter, to air out the house.

Air Fresheners

Nix em! Air fresheners actually pollute the air with phthalates (a chemical used to make fragrances last longer in products). My favorite way to freshen the air is to add a few drops of essential oil to water in a spray bottle, and then mist the air, draperies, and couch. If you must use air fresheners, opt for non-aerosol, all natural, hypoallergenic products such as Citrus Magic. If you are like me and adore candles, buy petroleum free candles made from beeswax or soy wax to limit the amount of soot and toxins you are adding to the air.

Lead

Get rid of it! Lead is a highly dangerous neurotoxin and is commonplace, a bad combination. It can be found in the paint of many houses and enters our lungs through chips and dust. The Environmental Protection Agency states that 80% of homes built before 1976 contain lead paint. It is especially dangerous for infants or anyone with a weak immune system. If you have an older home you should have your house professionally tested. If you do have lead, do not try to remove the paint yourself; call a specialist.

When it comes time to repaint, look for low VOC paints. Low VOC means that the paint contains fewer of the headache and cancer causing chemicals than regular paint. Brands include: Sherwin Williams, Benjamin Moore, AFM Safecoat, BioSheild, Anna Sova Luxury Organics, and Old Fashioned Milk Paint Co. Just ask the paint specialist at your local hardware store. (Not all lines of paint made by Sherwin Williams and Benjamin Moore are low VOC. It must say it specifically on the label.)

Flooring

Carpeting can be a breading ground of gross stuff such as mold, dust mites, allergens, and VOCs. If you can, remove that nasty stuff and opt

129

for hard floors made from sustainable ingredients. My favorite is bamboo flooring, as it comes in a huge variety of colors and is very durable. Other great options are hardwood from sustainably managed forests, cork, and linoleum. By the way, cork is naturally antibacterial, so go ahead and let your family members roll around on it! Look for the Forest Stewardship Council (FSC) label when purchasing wood.

If you must have something soft underfoot, use rugs because they can be easily cleaned without chemicals. Look for rugs made of wool, cotton, jute, hemp, alpaca fleece, banana fibers, and Nepalese cactus. Check out Odegard, Inc (www.odegardinc.com/flash/index.html) for rugs made of sustainable ingredients from Tibet and Nepal. The company also fights against child labor.

Here's a cool tip from **planetgreen.discovery.com**: You can use snow to clean a wool rug. Why? Freezing cold temperatures harden and break up bits of grease, and will also kill dust mites.

For a Moth Deterrent: Mix a few drops of lavender essential oil and cedar wood essential oil with water in a spray bottle, and mist clean clothes. You could also put cedar chips in a cotton bag and hang that near your clothes.

Room by Room: The Bedroom

For information on detoxing the nursery, please see the Babes and Babies section.

Beds

All mattresses sold in the United States are held to very stringent fire safety regulations. The fire retardants used in conventional mattresses include boric acid and antimony, which are identified as carcinogens. They are also made of petroleum-based polyester, nylon and polyurethane foam which give off dangerous volatile organic compounds (VOCs), which are associated with asthma, allergies, and other upper respiratory problems. Some mattresses are also treated with formaldehyde-emitting stain/water-repellants, which are also carcinogenic. The greenest option is to find a bed made of natural latex, wool and melamine. They do cost more, but are worth it for a better nights sleep. Examples include A Natural Home's Simply Affordable furniture line ($400+) and Savvy Rest ($1000+). A cheaper option is to buy a bed that uses fiber-based flame-retardant barriers and coil springs (less polyurethane foam). You can then buy an organic cotton mattress encasement or hypoallergenic cover to reduce your exposure to VOCs and dust mites. Make sure you air out your new bed, if it contains chemicals, for at least a week (preferably a month) prior to use.

Furniture and Décor

VOCs can be found in varnishes, finishes, glue, particleboard and MDF. Purchase furniture made from solid wood (FSC certified sustainable wood) or low-VOC materials and finishes. Antique furniture is also a great option. As cotton is one of the dirtiest crops when it comes to pesticides, opt for organic cotton whenever possible and other sustainable materials (hemp, bamboo) in your bedding and décor. See "Deadly Cotton" for more information. In my house, we use organic wool for our comforters and pillows because I have allergies and my husband tends to sweat when he sleeps. Wool is great for us because dust mites hate it, and it dries quickly. Check out **www.nontoxic.com** for organic, wool comforters. Opt for eco-friendly pillows stuffed with buckwheat or natural latex. Use low or no-VOC paint on your walls. Avoid mothballs, which are known to cause cancer in animals. Instead use cedar chips (or cedar furniture). Finally, avoid wall-to-wall carpeting and use rugs made of sustainable/natural materials.

Energy

Throw on an extra blanket and turn down the thermostat a few degrees in the winter. Try a programmable thermostat, which you can time to turn down in the evening and turn up in time to wake up. You will save energy, money and not have to worry about chilly toes first thing in the morn. You can also add storm panels to your windows to make them 50% more efficient. On occasion, open a window to ventilate the room.

By adjusting when your drapes are open and when they are closed, you can save money on heating and cooling. During the summer, open your windows and drapes at night to let in the cool night air. During the day, close your windows and drapes to keep the heat of the day from sneaking in. During the winter, open your drapes during the day to let the sunlight warm your home. As soon as the sun disappears (or your house is in the shade) close your drapes.

Romance

If you love using candles to create the perfect relaxing and romantic atmosphere, avoid traditional paraffin candles because they add soot and toxins to the air. Instead, opt for beeswax or soy wax candles that are scented with essential oils and do not have metal containing wicks. Try Bluewick candles, Luxe's beeswax candles, and It's a Soy candles. You can even try making your own. You can also install dimmer switches so you can easily have romantic lighting, and save electricity.

If you really want to turn up the romance, check out the Internet Shopping Guide for stores that sell eco-friendly sex toys and accoutrements. If you're crafty check out this book: Make Your Own Sex Toys: 50 Quick and Easy Do-It-Yourself Projects by Matt Pagett (2007).

Recipes and Resources

Cleaning Products

From our dishes to our clothes, floors, and even in the air, cleaning products are everywhere! We have turned tidiness into a war for spot-free sterility. We absorb these products and breathe them in, which is why it is so important not only for our health, but the health of our planet to use products that do not contain toxic chemicals. Don't use a nuclear bomb to annihilate a single germ! Instead of arming ourselves with petroleum-based cleaning products, there are plenty of natural and safe products and ways to keep your home clean and fresh.

Home Made Cleaning Products
Remember to ALWAYS label your homemade cleaning products with the name and ingredients to avoid cross contamination and dangerous mixes. Never mix ammonia and bleach.

All-purpose cleaner spray
2-tbsp vinegar
1-tsp borax
Very hot distilled water
¼-cup liquid soap or 1/8 cup liquid detergent
10-15-drops of essential oil to scent

You must mix these ingredients in the following order, other wise ingredients will clump and you will end up with muck. First, mix the vinegar with the borax in a 16 oz spray bottle. Next, fill the rest of the bottle with the hot distilled water. (It must be distilled or purified, because minerals found in undistilled water, like tap water and spring water, inhibit the cleaning power.) Then shake well until the borax is dissolved. If any clumps are left, they will clog the nozzle. Finally, add the liquid soap or detergent. (To scent, add the essential oils. If the soap/detergent is already scented, you might not want to add any essential oils.

Antiseptic Soap Spray
Distilled Water
3-tbsp liquid soap
20-30-drops of tea-tree oil for antiseptic

Fill the spray bottle up with the water first. Then add the liquid soap. If you do this in the opposite order, it will get sudsy. Add 20-30 drops of tea tree oil for antiseptic power. Shake to mix. This great for cleaning countertops!

Baking Soda
To clean bathtub rings, vanities, or remove stuck-on-food, sprinkle baking soda onto a damp sponge and scrub. For tougher spots, make a paste of baking soda and water; apply to the area and let sit for about 15 minutes.

To clear slow-running drains, pour ½ to ¾ cup baking soda and pour an equal amount of vinegar down the drain. 페이지: 134
Let stand at least 2 hours (best done overnight) and then flush with hot water. Do not use this method on blocked drains.

Borax
Borax is antifungal and a disinfectant. It is effective in removing dirt. You can use it in laundry or as a kitchen/bath cleaner.

Diaper Pail deodorizer and cleanser (Can also be used to deodorize trash cans)
Shaker container (I use an old baby powder container, clearly marked)
½-tsp tea tree oil
1-cup baking soda
Essential oils to scent (optional, I like to use eucalyptus or a mint)
Add the tea tree oil to the baking soda, stir very well, and work out lumps with a METAL fork. DON'T use plastic measuring spoons to measure the oils or they will dissolve, use metal. Sprinkle on diapers, in pail, or use to clean out pail.

Furniture Polish
1-cup olive oil
½-cup lemon juice

Mix in a spray bottle. Shake well and apply a small amount to a cleaning cloth. Spread evenly over furniture surface. Turn cloth to a dry side and polish dry. Don't use too much or it will take a while to dry.

Glass Cleaner
1-cup rubbing (isopropyl) alcohol
1-cup water
1-tablespoon white vinegar (use 1 tablespoon clear, non-sudsing ammonia instead for tougher jobs)

Mix in a spray bottle. Use.

Hydrogen Peroxide 3%
This is an excellent bleach alternative. It is antibacterial and helps remove stains.

Kitchen Cleanser Paste
Baking soda to fill half a container (I use an old butter container, clearly marked)
Lemon juice
Essential oil for fragrance (optional)

Fill the container half full with baking soda, slowly mix in lemon juice until you have a thick paste, then 15-20 drops of essential oil to scent. Mix well. Use to scrub just about any bathroom or kitchen surface. Let the paste sit for a bit on tough spots. Follow with the Vinegar Rinse. I suggest you only fill the container half way in case you make the mix too wet and need to add more baking soda.

Lemon Juice
Lemon juice can be used to clean soap scum, hard water deposits, brass and copper. You can also add it vinegar and baking soda to make a

scented cleansing paste. Save the peel to run through the garbage disposal. When you pass lemon peels through a disposal, it simultaneously cleans it and freshens the whole kitchen with the smell of citrus. Do the same with orange or lime peels.

Liquid Castile Soap
This is a great all-purpose cleaner and not only cuts grease, but disinfects as well. It is a staple ingredient of many organic body soaps and shampoos.

Olive Oil
Use this to polish furniture and to nourish real wood floors.

Table Salt
Add table salt to your natural cleaners to remove rust.

Undiluted White Vinegar
To clean the toilet, dump a bucket of water into the toilet to get the water level high enough to reach the sides where the water flushes in. Do not make it over flow. Pour undiluted white vinegar around the bowl and scrub with a toilet brush to remove stains and odor. Use a pumice stone to remove any remaining hard water rings. I usually then let it sit until for a few hours before I flush it all out.

To clean showerheads that have been clogged with mineral deposits, remove the showerhead and place in the sink or in a bowl. Add ¼ to ½ cup vinegar to the bowl (enough to cover the head of the showerhead. Let it stand for 2 hours to overnight, rinse and then buff to a shiny finish.

As fabric softener, add one cup of undiluted white vinegar to the laundry rinse cycle. It softens the clothes and cuts detergent residue.

You can use regular white vinegar for less tough problems, like cleaning countertops, toilet surfaces, and shower walls. Vinegar can also be used to polish brass.

Vinegar Rinse
Water
Vinegar
Essential oils to scent

Fill a spray bottle with equal parts water and vinegar; add essential oil scent of your choice. Shake. Spray on surface and then wipe with a dry towel.

How to make Soap Nuts liquid multipurpose cleaner

The following was provided by the Maggie's Soap Nuts website at **maggiespureland.com**. Soap Nuts liquid is great concentrated cleaner. Use it for washing humans and pets, fruit and vegetables, spot treating laundry, hand washing delicates, cleaning kitchens and bathrooms, washing cars and plants, repelling pests, cleaning jewelry, even sparking windows!

INSTRUCTIONS
Stove top method - Simmer 1 cup Soap Nuts on the stove in 4 cups water for 10 minutes. If the mixture suds and bubbles over, fear not! When cool, simply wipe off and find your stovetop squeaky clean! After 10 minutes, turn off heat, cover, and allow Maggie's Soap Nuts liquid to cool. When cool, mash the nuts with your hands. Strain the liquid into a bottle through a fine sieve or cheesecloth.

Soaking method - Soak 1 cup Maggie's Soap Nuts in 4 cups water overnight. In the morning, liquefy the mixture in your blender. Strain the liquid into a bottle through a very fine sieve or cheesecloth.

For more tips on how to use Maggie's Soap Nuts in your home, check out the Babe's Guide forum at **www.stephaniebyng.com**, click on Book Resources.

Resources

For more tips and tricks
(http://Planetgreen.discover.com)

Find eco-friendly services in your area
(www.Earth911.org)

For more information about soap nuts
(http://en.wikipedia.org/wiki/Sapindus)

For more information on sustainable living
(www.Sustainableisgood.com)

Bosch Appliances
(www.boschappliances.com) –
Makes energy efficient appliances.

Clean and Green natural cleaning recipes
(www.geocities.com/Heartland/Prairie/8088/clngrn.html)

Energy Star (www.energystar)

Forest Stewardship Council
(www.fsc.org)

Maggie's Soap Nuts
(www.maggiespurland.com)

Organized Home
(www.Organizedhome.com)

U.S. Dept of Energy WaterSense Program
(www.epa.gov/watersense)

An Eco-Babe Tip - Fruit Fly Trap

1 glass jar (I use pint sized)
1 metal canning ring
1 paper funnel (make your own)
Apple Cider Vinegar

Slip the funnel through the canning ring with the narrow end down. I sealed my funnel to the metal ring with glue. Pour a small amount of Apple Cider Vinegar into the jar, screw on the metal ring with funnel. Set near your produce that is attracting the flies. The flies are attracted to the vinegar and go down into the funnel but when they try to escape the jar they go "to the light" sorry for the pun, they climb the glass trying to get out and can not they will eventually drown in the vinegar.

-Linda Rushing, Sales Rep. Smyrna, TN

An Eco-Babe Business: Veriuni Earth sells family-safe cleaning products that are both effective and economical. I use the products and have been really impressed. I especially like the Basin, Tub and Tile cleanser. It has brought up some stains that were in our bathroom when we bought our house. I also, really like the Stain Treatment. Go to: tinyurl.com/3mtfa6 – **Linda Rushing, Sales Rep, Smyrna, TN**

An Eco-Babe Business: To me, green is more than just a color it is a way of life. I have been working with essential oils and herbs for the past 15 years. I am an educator, environmentalist and entrepreneur with two successful brands on the market. GreenTerpene.com and eoilco.com. – **Rachel Markel, College Professor-Miami Dade College, University Of Miami and Barry University. Miami, Florida.**

An Eco-Babe Business: Do you ever wish you had a personal assistant who knew the birthdays of all your friends and family and was ready to mail out your customized cards on time for every holiday and occasion? Now you can with our unique internet-based system (and these are NOT e-cards). Visit GreetingsByChristine.com today to learn more and to receive your FREE gift account. – **Christine Dew, Business Owner, Surprise, AZ**

My Personal Cleaning Regime

After all this, you may be wondering what I personally use. Remember, everyone is different, so you may need to experiment to find the organic products that are right for you.

- **Laundry** – Maggie's Soap Nuts (I boil them in water and add the infused water to an old laundry soap bottle. Then I just use the same amount of liquid as I would with conventional liquid laundry soap).
- **Laundry whites** – I just add baking soda to the wash cycle.
- **Fabric Softener** – Soap Nuts are pretty good at making laundry soft, but sometimes I will add a half cup of vinegar to the rinse cycle for extra softness.
- **Stain Remover** – Ecover Stain Remover (love the smell)
- **Countertops** – Water infused with lemon juice and Tea Tree Essential Oil, in a spray bottle.
- **Floor** – Ecover Floor Soap
- **Toilet** – Seventh Generation Toilet Bowl Cleaner (Minty!)
- **Bath/Shower** – Orange Cleaner
- **Daily Shower Spray** – Method Daily Shower Spray in ylang ylang
- **Dishwashing** – Seventh Generation Natural Dish Liquid (Lavender scented!)
- **Dishwasher** – Still shopping and using up Palmolive Eco. I can't wait to try something better.
- **Dusting** – I just use a slightly damp rag.
- **Carpets** – If they are particularly smelly, I dust them with baking soda and then let it set for about 15 minutes before vacuuming.
- **Windows** – I clean them with soapy water and wipe them with newspaper instead of a rag.
- **Just to smell nice** – I use a candle warmer, burn incense (I love it and can't stop), and light soy candles.

In writing this book, I have discovered many great brands and products and I can't wait to try them all. As I run out of each product, I will try something new and post reviews on my website at www.stephaniebyng.com.

Healthy Pets

Just like everything else we've addressed in this book so far, conventional products for pets have their dangers. Products such as flea collars, tick control products, and even soap contain dangerous chemicals and pesticides that are harmful not only for pets, but for us as well. They are especially toxic for pregnant women, and children who often have no problem rubbing their sweet little faces into their pet's fur. These have been documented by the Natural Resources Defense Council (NRDC). In 2000 the NRDC found that common pet products contained pesticides at a level 50,000 percent higher than the safe levels mandated by the Environmental Protection Agency (EPA). The products also contained some pesticides that act like neurotoxins. Because of this the NRDC is working to convince the EPA to ban all products using these pesticides. Most of the pesticides have been banned, but some continue to be used including one that is lethal in a large dose.

The statistics about pet deaths related to exposure to pesticides is not very clear, but it is estimated that thousands of pets have been injured or killed because of pesticides. So to keep your pets and family safe, avoid products that contain tetrachlorvinphos, carbaryl and propoxur. Other products to avoid include permethrin-based products, and tick-control products containing amitraz. Instead, try products that contain Lufenuron (Program®), methoprene (Nylar®) and pyriproxyfen (Biolar®). For more information, visit the NRDC website at www.nrdc. There is also a very informative product guide at www.greenpaws.org/products.php.

DIY Pet Care

You can avoid having to use a lot of fancy pet products by keeping up with your pet's grooming. By regularly combing, bathing and gently vacuuming your pet's fur, you can control your pet's fleas. Make sure you use a flea comb and if you see any fleas on the comb, drown them in soapy water. When you bathe your pet, you don't need to use fancy or conventional pet soap. Any organic soap that you use on your hair is just fine for your pet's hair. And with any soap, avoid getting it in your pet's eyes.

Some pets enjoy having their fur vacuumed with the hose attachment, some don't. Make sure your vacuum suction isn't super strong. Try to vacuum your home often and make sure you get under furniture and in crevices. If your vacuum uses bags, make sure you throw the bag away (outside) immediately to keep the fleas from escaping back into your house. The same goes for canister vacuums. I suggest you take the whole vacuum outside before you remove the canister or bag. If you have a severe infestation of fleas, you should have your carpets professionally steam cleaned. You could try cleaning the carpets yourself, but professionals can use hotter water and have a stronger suction. All kinds of gross things like to hang out on a wet carpet, so the quicker they dry, the better.

> Green Paws warns: If you suspect your pet or your child may have suffered negative health effects as a result of a flea product containing OPs or carbamates, consult with your veterinarian or your doctor immediately. If you think a child has been exposed a pesticide, call your local poison control center. Be sure to report all such incidents to the EPA's National Pesticide Telecommunications Network at 800-858- 7378. Let us know if you or someone you love (whether furry or not) has had a toxic reaction to a pet product, email us **greenpaws@nrdc.org.**

If your pet spends time outside, there are a few things you can do to reduce the likelihood of attracting fleas for your pet. First, cut your grass short and don't let your shrubs and bushes grow out of control. Second, sunlight keeps things from getting too moist, and fleas love moist areas, so make sure your pet's favorite spots get an ample amount of sunlight. Third, if that is not enough buy some nematodes (roundworms that can kick a ticks butt) from your garden center. They are chemical free and a natural way to control fleas. All you have to do is spread them around the area and let them get to work.

Finally, make sure you wash your pet's bedding once a week. Use hot water and be careful not to let the dirty bedding touch anything on its way to the washing machine. You could inadvertently spread flea eggs. Only use chemical flea treatments as a last resort and after consulting with your veterinarian.

Essential oils should be used sparingly to control fleas and ticks. Some people and pets are sensitive to them and can even cause severe allergic reactions. Do not use products containing pennyroyal oil as it has been known to cause comas, seizures and death in animals[43]. Safer alternatives include cedarwood, thyme, rosemary, lemongrass, and peppermint. I like to add just a few drops to my pet's bedding during the rinse cycle. You could also add a few drops to a spray bottle filled with water, and lightly mist the areas where your pet hangs out. When working with essential oils, be sure to DILUTE and watch for changes or signs of discomfort from your pet. If your pet shows signs of an allergic reaction, wash their bedding (or anything you sprayed) and take her/him to the vet.

Resources

Animal Welfare Institute (www.animalwelfareapproved.org) – Read about the new certification for humane animal treatment.
Green Paws (www.greenpaws.org)
Humane Society of the United States (www.hsus.org)
Natural Resources Defense Council (www.nrdc.org)
Society for Animal Protective Legislation (www.saplonline.org)

Renewable Power

Nowadays many people can choose their energy supplier. If you are one of those lucky people, pick a supplier who uses renewable energy. Wind, geothermal, solar and hydroelectric are all very good for the environment and are effective in supplying energy to your household. Find out if you are able to choose your energy supplier, by visiting Green-e's Pick Your Power Website at www.green-e.org/gogreene.shtml.

If you don't have a choice, you can do your part by paying a small green energy premium through your electric company or by purchasing carbon offsets. The way energy premiums work is that you voluntarily pay an additional amount on your electric bill and that money is then spent on creating renewable energy sources in your area. For example, my energy supplier is SRP (srpnet.com) and they allow you to pay a premium as low as $3 to fund community environmental projects. Projects have included solar power exhibits at the Phoenix Zoo, solar panels for parking structures and Park 'N' Ride. Carbon offsets are a way for you to make up for the pollution you create just by living (heating your home, running your car, the trash you create, etc). A dollar amount is calculated from your carbon footprint, and you would invest that amount in renewable energy. Learn more about carbon offsets and footprints at www.nrdc.org/globalwarming/offsets.asp.

RESOURCES

Alliance to Save Energy's Consumers Page
(www.ase.org/consumer/index.htm)
American Solar Energy Society (www.ases.org)
American Wind Energy Association (www.awea.org)
Atmosfair (www.atmosfair.com) – Invest in solar power for
developing countries.
Building with Awareness (www.buildingwithawareness.com)
California Energy Commission's Consumer Energy Center
(www.consumerenergycenter.org/)

Climate Counts (www.climatecounts.org) – See how major
   companies offset their carbon emissions.
Climate Friendly (www.climatefriendly.com) – Invest in renewable
   energy in Australia and New Zealand.
Energy Star Home Improvement Toolbox
   (www.energystar.gov/homeimprovement)
 Flex Your Power (www.fypower.org/)
Guide to Buying Clean Energy
   (www.nrdc.org/air/energy/gcleanen.asp)
Home Energy Magazine (www.homeenergy.org/)
Home Energy Saver (homeenergysaver.lbl.gov/)
My Climate (www.myclimate.org) – Invest in greenhouse, farms, and
   biomass facilities.
Native Energy (www.nativeenergy.com) – Calculate your carbon
   footprint and invest in offsets of wind-power and methane-gas
   energy.
Pick Your Power (www.green-e.org/your_e_choices/pyp.html)
Real Goods (www.realgoods.com)
Sun Lizard (www.alternativefuels.com.au)
The Insulation Fact Sheet (www.ornl.gov/sci/roofs)
U.S. DOE's Energy Savers Guide (www.eere.energy.gov/consumer/)

Composting: Not just for farmers!

Composting is going on around you all the time and just about everywhere. Composting is the decomposition of plant and dead materials into fertile dirt. Right under your feet, the forest floor is composting in action. The leaves pile up, decay, and eventually turn into dirt, which will nourish the surrounding roots. All of our household waste can be divided into three categories: recyclable, compost-able, and trash. Most of what we throw away can be recycled and/or composted, which leaves very little trash for our landfills. Yard and kitchen waste account for about 30% of the average American's trash.

Composting, when done correctly, will not attract rodents, does not smell and creates a great fertilizer for your houseplants or garden. It can even be done in an apartment!

There are many ways to compost. If you have open land, you can go bin-less and simply heap your compost in a pile on the ground or you can build an enclosure with pallets, studs, and/or plywood. There are even ready-made compost enclosures that you can purchase. Remember to contact your city to find out the regulations regarding composting, as some cities do not allow you to compost without an approved container.

If you don't have access to open land and are short on space, you can compost in a trashcan or buy a small ready-made composting container. Some cities provide free containers, so be sure to contact the waste management company in your area. For those of you who can't compost, research your area to see if there are any large-scale community composting projects, which will take your yard and kitchen wastes for free. Alternatively, you could even start up a compost group with some friends.

Once you understand the fundamentals, composting is easy and requires little effort.

The Basics

Good compost is like a good cake batter. With the proper ingredients, in the proper amount, you can make a great cake and the same goes for compost. Not to say that my cakes taste anything like fertilizer!

A proper compost heap provides an environment for microbes to live. Fungi, bacteria, worms, and insects digest the waste, so you want to make sure that the pile has enough air, water and food for them. The more maintained the heap, the more quickly your waste turns into compost.

Air

There are two types of microbes: aerobic and anaerobic. Aerobic microbes require air to do their jobs. Anaerobic microbes do not. The latter guys are what make a compost pile stink like rotting garbage. So you want to make sure that there is plenty of access to air in your pile. Straw, which doesn't mat down when wet, does a great job of keeping those airways open. If you're adding things such as grass, which clumps together and blocks air, make sure you mix it in thoroughly. It also helps to break up clumps of a single ingredient with a spade or garden fork. The goal is to keep your pile "fluffy" rather than compacted. The more you mix it, the less smelly it will be.

Water

Your pile needs to be damp at all times. The goal is to find a medium between too wet and too dry. It should be as moist as a wrung-out sponge. For example, you know it is too wet when your pile starts to mat down and smell like rotting garbage. If it's too dry, it will still decompose but at a much slower rate. If you accidentally get your pile too wet, just add dry ingredients, like leaves or straw, and mix thoroughly. If your pile is too dry, just add water and mix.

Food

The microbes eat your waste and need different types of food to have a balanced diet. Here is the food "pyramid" of microbes:

147

- 95% Browns – Dry and dead plant materials (autumn leaves, wood chips, saw dust, dead plants, pine needles, ground corn cob). Browns make up the carbon that the microbes need for energy.
- 5% Greens – Fresh and green (live) plant materials (fruit/vegetable scraps, fresh plants, coffee/tea grounds, fresh manure). Greens make up the nitrogen that the microbes need.
- Activator

The proper mix of browns and greens help maintain the right amount of air and water in the pile. An activator is an ingredient that contains both nitrogen and protein, which speeds up decomposition. It's not necessary if you maintain the right percentage of browns vs. greens, but it doesn't hurt either. As an apartment dweller, I don't have access to a lot of brown material; as such I use an activator to keep my pile healthy. Every time I add an ingredient, I dust the pile with an activator and then moisten it slightly. The best activator is alfalfa meal, which can be found at any feed or garden store. Other options include Litter Green (cat litter made from alfalfa meal), bone meal, cottonseed meal, blood meal, rich soil, or barnyard manure. Also, keep in mind that a varied diet will lead to better soil, so experiment with your ingredients.

Suggested Materials

Apple pomace
Birdcage cleanings
Brewery wastes
Cannery wastes
Castor bean pomace
Chaff
Cheese whey
Cocoa bean hulls
Coffee grounds and filters
Corncobs and husks
Dryer Lint

Dust from vacuum cleaner
Eggshells
Evergreen needles
Feathers
Felt waste
Flower arrangements
Freezer burned vegetables
Garden waste (dead plants, carrot tops, corn stalks, etc)
Grape pomace
Grass clippings

Hair
Hay
Kitchen wastes
Leather
Leaves
Leftovers (without meat)
Lint (Stuff you sweep off floor)
Mail (shredded paper)
Manures (horse, cow, goat, pig, rabbit, poultry)
Matches
Milk, sour and soy
Moldy cheese
Nut shells
Old Fruit
Old Vegetables
Old food as long as it doesn't contain meat
Paper Napkins/Towels

Peanut hulls
Pine needles
Pond weeds
Popcorn
Potato Peels
Sawdust and shredded bark (use sparingly, and not from pressure treated wood)
Seaweed, kelp, eelgrass
Spices
Stale Bread, chips, pasta
Straw
Sugar cane
Tobacco stems
Toenail clippings
Weeds
Wood ash
Wood chips and rotted wood

If you get creative, you can find many great ingredients for free. Most grocery stores will give you unsellable or expired fruits and vegetables for free. Just bring your own container. Ask your neighbors if you can have their leaves and lawn clippings. Hair contains a lot of nitrogen and can give your compost a boost. For daring babes, ask your local barber or beautician for the days hair clippings.

Ingredients to avoid

Animal bones
Animal waste (flesh)
Bermuda grass
Buttercup
Cat/dog litter/feces
Charcoal briquettes
Chicken Manure
Coal ash

Diseased garden plants
English Ivy
Eucalyptus
Grease
Human waste
Magnolia leaves
Morning glory

Newspaper (some have inks with toxins. Call paper to find out)

Noxious weeds

Nut grass

Oil

Sawdust (use sparingly, and not from pressure treated wood)

Woody material that can't be broken down.

Other Considerations

Compost piles may go dormant in the winter, but will start back up when the temperature rises.

Compost piles will decompose faster if they are hot, but it is not a necessity. Nitrogen rich ingredients are what heat up a compost pile. As long as you have a good mix with proper aeration and moisture, it will decompose just fine at 50°F/10 °C or hotter. If your pile is small it may be cooler by default as the pile is not big enough to insulate itself. You need about three cubic feet of ingredients for it to insulate itself. If you have a cooler pile, you can add red worms, which will help with the decomposition. You can get those at any bait shop or pet store.

You know your compost is ready to be used when it is dark and has a sweet earthy smell. It should be so decomposed that you can't identify one ingredient from another. You may see a few bits of brown ingredients like straw and leaves, which is fine for outdoor gardens. With seedlings, you will want the compost to be very well decomposed.

There are several uses for compost. You can cultivate it into garden soil prior to planting. It can be added to the bases of plants during the growing season. You can sprinkle it on the lawn. It can be used as food for houseplants. Compost can even be used as mulch.

Composting Systems

Single Bin Systems

A single bid system is the easiest one for those new to composting and those who are not looking to make a lot. All you need is an enclosure of at least 3 cubic feet. If you are making your own with pallets, wire or cinder blocks, you should make it 3 feet wide. You can often find wooden pallets behind stores, but make sure you ask before you take them. More than likely you will build your pile over time, which means the stuff on the bottom will decompose first because it's the oldest. When the compost on the bottom is finished, you will need to take the fresh stuff off the top and set it aside to remove the finished compost at the bottom.

If you are short on space, you can also use a trashcan. This will also lessen the chance of rodents getting in. I prefer galvanized metal or heavy-duty polyethylene cans. To use these, just make sure you can lock or strap down the lid. You will also need to punch ¼ inch holes all over the can (sides and bottom) and lid for aeration. Put the can on top of a few bricks or cinder blocks so that it can drain properly, and place in an area where the drainage will not do damage to any structures. I mention drainage because when you water your compost, you need to allow for the excess water to go somewhere, as opposed sitting at the bottom. If you want, you could collect this drainage and re-apply it to the compost later. As you fill the can, cover each layer of waste with a bit of soil or activator. To keep the can from smelling, you will need to stir the ingredients a bit more often than you would with a pallet or chicken wire bin.

Multi-Bin Systems:

This is very similar to the single bin system, except you have two or three bins in a row. The purpose of a multi-bin system is that once the 1st bin is full, you can leave it to decompose while you start to fill another bin. By the time the 2nd bin is full, the 1st bin is usually ready to use. I suggest you start with a single bin and if it looks like it is going to be full before it is done composting then you can easily add another. Most people will not need more than 2 bins.

Rotating Systems

If you are looking to invest in an easy, quick composting system, you can purchase a rotating system. They are a bit small but when used properly, can create compost in less than a month. You fill it about ¾ full with a mix of greens and moist browns and give the unit a turn every day. This will aerate the ingredients for you. You will, however, need to have a separate bucket/container to put your waste in while the unit is composting. When the batch in the unit is done, you simply dump it out and add the new waste.

(Photo courtesy Planet Natural
www.planetnatural.com)

Commercial Systems

Commercial systems are more expensive than the build-it-yourself kind, but they have added conveniences. The Planet Natural store sells units that vary from those specially made for urban use to large-scale farm use. They also sell products designed to speed up the decomposition process. They also allow you to compost in colder climates as they insulate the materials, as well as keep rodents out. While they are an instant solution, they perform relatively the same as anything you could build on your own. Just make sure you purchase one made from recycled materials, to support manufacturers that recycle.

Vermicomposting

This is a fancy word for worm bin composting. You can use special containers and some are completely enclosed so you can keep them indoors if you like. However, you don't have to purchase any special container, as the worms can be turned loose on a pile with no ill effects. Vermicomposting requires a special kind of worm. Garden-variety earthworms will not do. You need a special type that is adapted to living in decomposing materials such as Eisenia foetida and Lumbricus rubellus. They are also known as red worm, manure worm or red wiggler. You can find them at bait shops and some pet stores. Make sure you write down all the previous names, in case the store clerk doesn't know their Latin name. If you don't want to chance buying the wrong kind, you can mail order them from a composting website. I suggest The Worm Farm (**www.thewormfarm.com**).

Vermicomposting is a little bit different than regular composting, so I suggest you check out some of the websites listed at the end of the chapter. They need cool, moist bedding in the form of brown ingredients, with green ingredients buried in the bedding. If the pile is too packed, it will be difficult for the worms to move around.

Resources

- Appelhof, Mary. *Worms Eat My Garbage*
- Campbell, Stu. *Let It Rot!*
- Harmonious Press (publisher) *Backyard Composting*
- Jenkins, J.C. *The Humanure Handbook*

City Farmer (www.Cityfarmer.org)
Cornell composting
    (Compost.css.cornell.edu/Composting_homepage.html)
Solid Waste (www.Solidwate.org/composting)
Clean Air Gardening (www.Cleanairgardening.com)
Planet Natural (www.Planetnatural.com)
The Worm Farm
    (www.thewormfarm.com)

An Eco-Babe Tip:
I keep a small "herd" of eisenia fetida in the kitchen in a Styrofoam "ice chest". I drilled a few air supply holes in its top, and stapled a scrap of plastic window screen inside to block the insects and would-be escaping worms. It's not stinky. Sometimes there's a faint odor like you'd have walking through a wooded area outdoors. If it gets "whiffy" I lay a paper towel over the box (loosely). - **Marian Pearn, age 71, retired teacher/counselor, grandmother and putterer, Flower Mound, TX**

Recycling

Do you care about what happens to your garbage after it's whisked away from your driveway? While it may disappear from your mind, it doesn't disappear from the earth. It's either hidden in a landfill or burned; yet with concerns about overfilling landfills and air pollution, we have to do something else. This is where recycling comes in. It's more than just separating cans and plastic. According to the Energy Information Administration, in 2003, Americans generated 236 million tons of garbage! Recycling is smart. It saves money, natural resources, energy, and the rain forest.

Getting Started

The first thing you want to do is contact your city hall, sanitation department, recycling office or waste management company to find out about recycling services in your area. Some places collect your recyclables for free; others pay you and others charge you. Some have curbside pickup, recycling drives, drop off locations or buyback centers.

Questions to ask your recycling center:

When are you open?
What materials to you accept? (Some places don't take glass.)
How do you want the materials sorted or packaged?
How clean do the materials have to be?
Do you pay for materials and how much?

Setup

Rather than separating your trash the day before it's picked up, it's best to setup a system in your house that doesn't involve digging or resorting.

Take a look at your trash and see if there are any items that you commonly throw away that could be recycled. This is a good time to check out your shopping habits to see if buying soda in cans, rather than

155

plastic bottles (or vice versa) is better for you. Or if your recycling center doesn't accept glass, for example, you can alter your shopping habits to avoid glass containers. When you're just starting out, it's important to take it easy to avoid feeling overwhelmed. Take the time to come up with a plan. How often will you dispose of your recyclables (once a week, once a month, etc)? What kind of container will you use (trash bags, bins, stacking containers)? How big do your containers need to be? Make sure you don't use containers so big that you can't easily lift and move them. You will also want to make sure they can easily fit in your car. Where will you keep your containers (under the sink, outside, garage, pantry)?

Container Ideas

Paper/plastic bags
Cardboard boxes
Milk crates
Plastic baskets
Rattan baskets

Trashcans with lids
Potato sacks
Recycling storage units
Plastic stacking bins

I made my recycling setup a work of art. I bought a couple white kitchen trashcans with the pop-up lid and foot pedal and lined them up on a wall. I then took the time to paint each one. For example, the trashcan lid was painted with splashes of several reddish paints with an image of a woman putting something in a can painted in the middle. The cardboard-can lid was painted with splashes of green and blue with a recycling symbol in the middle. They look cool so I don't mind them being seen in my kitchen. I sort as I go, so I don't have to do any separating later. I also don't purchase anything in a glass or aluminum container. I try to buy all of my beverages in recyclable plastic. It helps that I don't drink soda. I currently use plastic bags to line my cans, but I plan on making my own cloth liners for the recycling bins in the near future. That way I take the cloth bags to the recycling center, rather than the bins.

How to Sort

The wealth of information available on recycling obviously won't fit into a single chapter, so I highly suggest you check out the resources at the end. Here are some general tips.

- Before you crush your aluminum cans, find out how your recycling center accepts them.
- Separate tin (canned goods) from aluminum (soda) cans.
- Separate your glass containers by color: clear, green and brown. If the glass is even slightly colored, do not put it in with the clear. If you have other colored glass, put it with the color it's closest to; i.e. darker colors in brown and lighter colors in green.
- Separate paper by color and type. Remove all paperclips and staples, plastics (windowed part of envelopes) as well as glued parts (like labels or post-it notes sticky section).
- Newspaper, glossy magazines and cardboard are not to be mixed with paper. Each needs to be separate.
- Plastic is numbered 1-7 (check the bottom of containers). Separate them by number. If it's number 7, it's not recyclable. Call your recycling center to see what types of plastic they accept, and then alter your shopping habits accordingly. Try to buy only #1 as it is easily recycled into all kinds of products from carpets to car bumpers.
- Waxed milk and soy cartons are not recyclable. Try to purchase them in number 1 or 2 plastic or glass.

The following are considered Hazardous and require special handling. Contact your hazardous waste facility.

Adhesives	Drain Cleaners	Lead
Aerosol Cans	Electronics	Lighter Fluid
Air Fresheners	Explosives	Liquid Cleaners
Asbestos	Fire Extinguisher	Medical Waste
Car Batteries	Freon	Medical Sharps
Car Fluids	Furniture Polish	Medications
CFLs	Kerosene/Propane	Mercury

Mercury	Paint Thinners	Rust Removers
Thermostats	Pesticides	Shoe Polish
Metal Polishers	Photographic	Single Use
Mothballs	Chemicals	Batteries
Motor Oil	Pool Chemicals	Smoke Detectors
Nail Polish	Rechargeable	Styrofoam
Remover	Batteries	Wax Coated Milk
Oven Cleaners	Rug/upholstery	Cartons
Paint	Cleaners	

Remember just about EVERYTHING can be recycled, from your old phones and fax machines, to your clothes and old appliances. Use the resources below to find out how.

Resources

Donald, Rhonda Lucas. *Recycling (True Books: Environment)*
Guillain, Charlotte. *Reusing and Recycling (Help the Environment)*
Inskipp, Carol. *Reducing And Recycling Waste (Improving Our Environment)*
Lund, Herbert F. McGraw-Hill *Recycling Handbook, 2nd Edition*
Richard, Porter C. The Economics of Waste
The Earth Works Group. *The Recycler's Handbook*
Wong, Janet S. and David Roberts. *The Dumpster Diver*

- Earth 911 (www.Earth911.org) – This website has just about all the information you need. You can even find your municipal hazardous waste facility just by entering your zip code.
- Environmental Protection Agency (www.Epa.gov)
- Global Recycling Network (www.Grn.com)
- Recycle your old electronics (www.recycles.org), (www.pcsforschools.org) or (www.eiae.org)
- Starfish Project (www.thestarfishproject.org) – They take your unwanted medications and distribute them to developing countries who can't afford them.

Freecycling

Would you like to get stuff you need for free? Would you like to make sure that your used items find a good home? Well then Freecycling is for you. Freecycle is an organization dedicated to keeping things out of landfills. It is about extending the usefulness of items by giving them away to someone who needs it. Freecycling is not about charity, helping the poor, getting a bunch of free stuff, making money, or advertising businesses and services. Freecycle is a community that wants to spread environmental awareness. There is a wide variety of items offered and wanted on Freecycle, from old doors, to moving boxes, to shoes.

How it works
You apply for membership in the Freecycle group in your community. If you have things you no longer need, you post an offer on the message board. You chose who you want to gift your item to. No one is under any obligation to give their gift to anyone based on their financial status, size of family, or personal story. If you have a need, you post a wanted message on the board. This is a request for a gift and if someone happens to have what you need, and wants to give it to you, then they will contact you via email. If someone is offering something that you need, you simply respond to their offer via email. If the chose to gift it to you, then you arrange a time to pick it up. It's as simple as that.

There are a few rules. First, everything posted must be free and legal. You are not allowed to charge, or barter/trade for goods and services. Also, everything posted must be appropriate for all ages. You are also asked to be patient and polite. If you are interested in joining a Freecycle group in your area, please visit **www.freecycle.**

Babes with Babies

It's amazing how a little bundle of joy can leave such a huge impact on the environment.

From mountains of disposable diapers to barely used clothing and entire rooms full of toys, children consume millions of tons of natural resources and contribute to overflowing landfills before they are even able to say 'global warming.'

Modern parenthood is consumerism at its worst. It's gluttony with a stork.

So as An Eco-Mommy, what are you to do?

How Green Is Your Baby?

Take this quick yes/no quiz to see how green you children are. To see how much you have improved, take this quiz now and after you have made some positive changes. This allows you to quantify how green you have made your children and keep track of areas for future improvement.

- ❑ Do you believe labels that say "natural" or "organic"?
- ❑ Do you know what elimination communication is?
- ❑ Do you know what VOCs are?
- ❑ Do you know what fair trade is?
- ❑ Do you know what your baby's toys, clothes, bedding, diapers are made of?
- ❑ Are your soft toys made out of certified organic/sustainable and fair-trade fabrics?
- ❑ Do you buy your toys used or from green stores?
- ❑ Do you avoid purchasing battery operated toys?
- ❑ Do you avoid purchasing plastic toys and teethers?
- ❑ Do you use cloth diapers?
- ❑ Do you use cloth wipes?
- ❑ Do you use certified organic linens and towels?
- ❑ Do you use eco-friendly laundry soap?
- ❑ Do you wash your laundry with cold water?
- ❑ Do you line dry your babies diapers?
- ❑ Do you use eco-friendly or homemade household cleaners?
- ❑ Do you read the labels on your baby's bath and body products?
- ❑ Do you use certified organic or homemade creams/lotions on your baby?
- ❑ Do you use certified organic or homemade body care products on your baby?
- ❑ Does you baby sleep with you or in an organic bed?
- ❑ Do you avoid wall-to-wall carpeting in your home?
- ❑ Are you using used or eco-friendly furniture in your nursery?

- ❑ Is your baby's room painted with Low/No VOC paint or covered with bamboo wallpaper?
- ❑ Do you make your own baby food?

- ❑ Are your children on an organic diet?
- ❑ Are you using glass, stainless steel or BPA free bottles and sippy cups?
- ❑ Do you make no-trash lunches for your kids?

Dangerous Disposable Diapers

Just like disposable menstrual products, disposable diapers are linked with major health and environmental problems. If it's bad to put a toxic pad against your vagina, imagine how bad it is against a baby's sensitive skin. Here are some of the main concerns with disposable diapers.

Health

Just like menstrual pads, disposable diapers contain traces of dioxin, which we know is a by-product of bleaching[44]. I must reiterate again, that the bleaching process is done just to make the product look clean and white, and does not sanitize. Dioxin is extremely toxic, is linked to cancer and is banned in most countries[45]. Disposable diapers also contain Tributyl-tin, which is linked to hormone problems, and sodium polyacrylate, which is linked to the toxic shock syndrome outbreak of the 1980s[46].

A study by the Archives of Disease in Childhood published in 2000[47], found that boys who wear disposable diapers for a prolonged period showed increased scrotal temperature, which can affect and even stop the natural cooling process that is important for sperm production.

Until the 1940s, when rubber and plastic pants were introduced, diaper rash was almost unheard of. Too much moisture against the skin is the common cause of diaper rash. Another cause of rash is skin sensitivity, as some babies are allergic to the synthetic materials in diapers[48]. I was one of those babies.

Environment

Did you know you are supposed to empty out the feces from diapers into the toilet before you throw them away? Less than half of a percent (.05%) of diaper waste makes it into the sewage system. This leaves about 5 million tons of untreated feces, possibly carrying over 100 intestinal viruses, sitting in our landfills and seeping into groundwater. It also attracts disease-ridden insects and rodents[49]. If you want to learn more about feces and urine in landfills, read this report by the Environmental Protection Agency
http://www.epa.gov/osw/nonhaz/municipal/pubs/98charac.pdf

In 1990, almost 20 years ago, 18 billion disposable diapers where thrown away every year in the United States[50]. You can be sure that number has risen substantially. In a household with children in diapers, the diapers make up over 50% of that household's waste[51]. Out of all the things we throw away, disposable diapers are the third largest item in landfills.

What does it take to make disposable diapers for one baby? Every year, it takes 300 pounds of wood, 50 pounds of petroleum feedstock (oil), and 20 pounds of chlorine. That's one baby for one year. Despite our current energy crisis, we are wasting 3.4 billion gallons of oil to make disposable diapers. In addition to that, we spend over $300 million dollars a year just to discard disposable diapers, and it takes possibly 500 years for the diapers to decompose[52].

Interesting fact: Number of disposables used per day in 1994: Australia uses 2.2 million, Japan 6.7 million, the UK 9 million, and the U.S. 49 million[53]. To put this into perspective, the U.S. population is only double that of Japan.

Personal Cost

Conservative estimates show that the average child uses about 6,000 to 8,000 diapers until they are fully potty trained. This means that the total cost to diaper a child through potty training, depending on whether you use generic or name-brand diapers, is between $2,000 and $5,000

Biodegradable diapers

Biodegradable diapers are made with plant-based plastics, which mean they do not contain oil products like normal disposable diapers. They are supposed to be compostable; however they have been found unable to break down in landfills, due to improper composting conditions. They will compost in a composting toilet, in a vermicompost pile, or a very well maintained compost pile. However, you would have so many diapers that you would need to have a very large composting heap. Some biodegradable diapers are flushable. For more information check out **Gdiapers.com** and **Eenee.com.**

Cloth Diapers

Cost

Most cloth diapers will last through multiple children, and even after that they can be used as rags. Most families need 3-6 dozen cloth diapers, depending on how often they wash them and how many children are using them. Prices vary, but most families can purchase all the cloth diapers they will ever need for about $300. Prices can vary to $1000, but that is usually for extra bells and whistles.

The non-profit organization, Real Diaper Association, which educates families about disposable and cloth diapers, has gathered data from the U.S. Census Bureau about the national costs of disposable diapering. Based on their research[54], about 9.5 million children are using diapers at any one time. Previous studies have shown that 92.5% of these children wear disposable diapers. This means that about 8.8 million children are using about 28 billion disposable diapers a year. At the lowest estimate of about $800 a year for disposable diapers per child, it is estimated that, as a nation, we spend about 7 billion dollars every year. If every single one of those children were switched to cloth diapers, we would save over 6 billion dollars. That is enough to feed 2.5 million American children for an entire year, which coincidentally is roughly the amount of children under the age of 6 who live in poverty in the United States[55].

There are two standard systems of cloth diaper. The first are diapers with separate waterproof covers. The second are called all-in-one or AIO diapers that have the waterproof cover sewn on. Both systems can be made more absorbent by adding liners. What varies in these systems are the fabric and style.

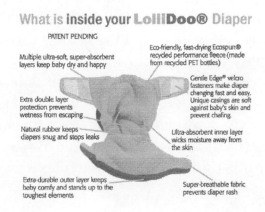

What is inside your LolliDoo® Diaper

PATENT PENDING

Multiple ultra-soft, super-absorbent layers keep baby dry and happy

Extra double layer protection prevents wetness from escaping

Natural rubber keeps diapers snug and stops leaks

Extra-durable outer layer keeps baby comfy and stands up to the toughest elements

Eco-friendly, fast-drying Ecospun® recycled performance fleece (made from recycled PET bottles)

Gentle Edge® velcro fasteners make diaper changing fast and easy. Unique casings are soft against baby's skin and prevent chafing.

Ultra-absorbent inner layer wicks moisture away from the skin

Super-breathable fabric prevents diaper rash

Fabric

There are so many different fabric combinations for cloth diapers that it can be daunting trying to choose the right one for your baby. As you are saving so much money by cloth diapering, don't be afraid to experiment and try more than one. There are many websites where you can sell your gently used cloth diapers, so you can easily dispose of diapers that didn't work for you. Check out **www.diaperswappers.com, www.ebay.com, www.diapertraders.com, www.clothdiaperexchange.com, and www.diaperjungle.com.**

For the absorbent layer, it's best to avoid any synthetic fibers as they repel moisture. Most parents opt for cotton, or hemp. Some feel that unbleached and organic fabrics work and feel best. Egyptian cotton is loved for its luxuriousness, terry for its durability and flannel for its softness. Hemp fleece is loved for being all of the above. Twill is often used in prefold (explained below) diapers. Polyester fleece is commonly used as the top layer fabric because it pulls the moisture away from the baby's body.

165

Diaper covers also come in an array of fabric choices. Some companies are even using science to create new fabrics out of recycled materials. Cover fabrics need to be waterproof to be viable. Wool is commonly used because it breathes well, but it needs to be re-waterproofed every few weeks. Wool contains lanolin oil, which washes out over time, so you just have to add the lanolin back in. Some brands use PUL (polyurethane laminated fabric), but it does contain some toxic chemicals. Parents like it because it is maintenance free, however it doesn't breathe as well as wool. Better options, where you don't have to choose between comfort, toxicity, and ease of use are being created as we speak. (Check out the Eco-Babe Business at the end of the chapter that is using soda bottles to make diapers!)

Style

Prefold – These are standard flat rectangular diapers. I was raised in these, and my mother is still using them as cleaning rags! They have been improved since then and pins are no longer required. All you need are covers that come in a wrap style that holds the prefold in place and then you just fasten the cover over them. Check out the brands Bummis, Prorap, or Lambkin.

Contoured – This style does not require any folding. They are shaped like an hourglass and sit inside the wrap style covers.

Fitted – These have Velcro, tie or snap closures that allow you to make sure you have a snug fit. These still require a cover.

AIO – (All-in-One) These diapers have the waterproof layer sewn to the outside, so you don't need a cover. These are great diapers to leave with babysitters, and extended family, as they are easy to use. Check out Bumkins. They don't work as well as other styles for overnight or heavy use. They can also take longer to dry and cost more.

Accessories

No, I'm not talking about handbags and necklaces. Accessories for cloth diapering include liners, doublers and wipes. Liners and doublers are extra pads that you fold and place in the diaper for added absorbency. These are great for overnight and heavy use. They come in rectangle and hourglass shapes. They may not be necessary, as it depends on your child. Wipes can be small washcloths or cut up sheets/shirts/fabric. They are used to clean the baby between changes. As you don't want to scrub your baby with a dry cloth, make up a simple wipe solution of warm water and maybe a few drops of essential oil. Tea Tree oil is antibacterial, and lavender or peppermint is soothing. Always use essential oils sparingly as some babies are sensitive to them. Dilute, Dilute, Dilute!

Shopping

It's difficult to find cloth diapers in stores. However, I just heard that Target is now selling Bumkins. The problem with this is that you are not given many fabric, style and size options. Your best bet it to check out the numerous online stores, many of which are run by work-at-home moms (WAHMs). **Check out the shopping guide in the appendices.**

Cleaning

Cloth diapers are easier to clean and maintain than most people think. All you need is a waterproof diaper bag and the proper soaps. Empty the poop into the toilet and use toilet paper to scrape it off if you have to. Squirt the diaper with BacOut (http://www.bi-o-kleen.com/general.htm), which is a natural odor and stain eliminator, and then toss it into the dirty diaper bag. Every few days wash them. Some parents will give them a cold rinse to prevent stain setting and then wash them in hot water. Do not use bleach or fabric softener. If you have stains, just set the diapers out in the sun to bleach naturally. I also suggest that you pour in a half cup of vinegar during the rinse cycle to avoid soap build up. This is also a natural fabric softener. If you don't want to wash your diapers, search the Internet for a local diaper service.

Resources

Diaper Pin *(*www.diaperpin.com*)* - Visit us and learn what kinds of cloth diapers are out there, read up on tips and tricks for easy diaper care, and find out where to buy them
Real Diaper Association (www.realdiaperassociation.org)

Gross-loh, Christine (2007) *The Diaper-Free Baby: The Natural Toilet Training Alternative*
Murray, Geralyn Broder (2008) *The Light at the End of the Diaper Pail: Inspiration for New Motherhood*
Quick Easy Guides (2008) *How To Use a Cloth Diaper*
Taviano, Marla (2008) *Changing Your World One Diaper at a Time: A Reflective Journey Through Your Baby's First Year*

An Eco-Babe Tip:

When I had my first son, I thought about cloth diapering, but was extremely overwhelmed with all the options and gave up before I ever got started-prefolds, fitteds, pockets, all-in-ones, wraps, soakers, it just made my head spin. Around the time my son turned a year old, we found out we were expecting our second child. As I had chosen to leave my career as a paralegal and stay home with my son, finances were a little tight and having two children in diapers would be quite an expense, so I decided to take the time and figure out what modern cloth diapering was all about. When I told my mom what I was thinking about doing, she started to laugh. "I used cloth diapers with you and trust me, you will get sick of diaper pins and plastic pants after a day", she said. What I discovered was a cloth-diapering world as different as night and day from the cloth-diapering world my mom knew. While some still use prefolds with pins and plastic pants, those are far from your only options! I discovered the convenience of disposable diapers with the cost savings and environmental benefits I was looking for in cloth diapers. Even my husband (who hated diaper changes the way most kids hate eating vegetables) was excited to give these 'cloth things' a try. All it took was our first order of 3 pocket style diapers and we were hooked. Now, two years and another baby later, we have tried every style and type of diaper and cover (and now cloth training pants) out there. I can really say I don't have a preference as to one system or type of diapering. We have never regretted our switch to cloth and love to talk about it with anyone and everyone. Yep, my motorcycle riding, car wrenching, avid sportsman of a husband loves to talk about cloth diapers! As dads are usually more than half the battle in convincing people to make the change, his advocacy has probably done more for the world of cloth diapering than I will ever do.

If I can help parents find what works for them and get them to make the switch to cloth, then I consider that a huge success for that family, for the cloth diapering community and for our entire planet. We really are changing the world for our kids one cloth diaper at a time. - **Megan Christensen, Work at Home mom of 2 and one on the way, Kingman, AZ**

An Eco-Babe Business Spotlight: LolliDoo®

"Born from our personal desire to use eco-friendly and safe diapers for our own babies, LolliDoo® fills the gap between land-filling disposable diapers and uncomfortable traditional cloth diapers," explains Alison Manes, co-founder of GGSI and co-creator of LolliDoo® diapers. Her co-founder and co-creator, Melissa Morgan adds, "Parents no longer have to sacrifice their baby's happiness for an eco-friendly, green diaper solution."

The two founders, who met through an online parenting website in 2004, quickly found that they shared similar values on natural parenting and became fast friends. Determined to make cloth diapers more environmentally and baby friendly, they researched and developed their ideas over the next few years.

Comprising most cloth diapers, cotton becomes cold and clammy when saturated with moisture, certainly not the most effective – or comfortable - way to keep baby dry. Inspired by the high-performance outdoor adventure clothing industry, LolliDoo® Diapers utilize a high-tech fabric that actually wicks moisture away from the skin toward the breathable outer layer, where air circulates to dry any accumulating moisture. The ultra-soft performance fleece is made from recycled PET (polyethylene terephthalate) plastic bottles (commonly used for soft drinks and water) and is the most eco- and baby-friendly fiber available. Each LolliDoo® Diaper is made from a minimum of 6 PET bottles, keeping bottles - as well as disposable diapers - out of landfills. The recycling of PET also saves millions of barrels of oil each year.

LolliDoo® is also better for baby because it doesn't have the toxic waterproof outer layer of polyurethane laminated fabric (PUL) found in most traditional cloth diapers. The patent-pending LolliDoo® Diapers quickly pull moisture away from the skin, leaving baby drier and cleaner. The five ultra-soft, super-absorbent layers are also highly breathable, which helps prevent uncomfortable diaper rash. The outer layer has been specially designed with unique air pockets that keep baby warm, snug and comfortable during all types of weather, without the bulk of traditional insulating fabrics.

Velcro fasteners – designed so they won't attach to other fabrics - make diaper changing a snap, while Gentle Edge® Velcro casings protect baby from chafing. A natural rubber elastic provides for a truly customizable fit - keeping diapers snug and preventing leaks.

The 100% machine-washable LolliDoo® Diapers release messes immediately, and save precious resources by thriving in cold-water washing - emerging from the spin cycle almost completely dry. Unlike other cloth diapers, LolliDoo® diapers just need a few minutes in the dryer or on the line, and they're ready to wear.

Co-founder and inventor Melissa Morgan explains, "Our tests of extreme diapering conditions (toddlers and overnight use) show that despite large quantities of urine, baby's bottom is as dry as it was when the diaper was first put on. As mothers, we tend to like that."

LolliDoo is available online at http://www.lollidoo.com and will also be sold at select retail stores.

About Go Green Sustainable Industries (GGSI), LLC
Born from their desire to use eco-friendly and safe diapers for their own babies, Alison Manes and Melissa Morgan created GGSI and the LolliDoo® line of re-usable, all-in-one cloth diapers, complementary wetbags and wipes. In the next few years, the company plans to add other eco-friendly products and services that focus on families and education. The founders are committed to ensuring that all of their products are handcrafted in the USA with eco-friendly, sustainable and ethically processed materials, and that all aspects of the GGSI business are run with respect to minimizing environmental impact. They are also developing a recycling program that allows consumers to return the

diaper to them at the end of its useful life, where they'll feed it into existing fiber recycling channels.

GGSI's websites (http://www.ggsillc.com and http://www.lollidoo.com) also offer a variety of informative articles, tips, resources/links and message forums for the health and eco-conscious parent.
– Originally written by Alison Manes, modified and used with permission.

The Lil' Yummy Tummy

Infants and young children are more vulnerable to toxins because their bodies and brains grow the fastest between the ages of 0 - 3 years. Their immune, central nervous and hormonal systems are particularly susceptible to damage from toxins. Non-organic baby food is often made of condensed fruits/vegetables that may include concentrated amounts of pesticides. Some pesticides are linked with reduced intelligence when fetuses are exposed to them in the womb. This happens when pesticides ingested by the mother are passed to the fetus through the mother's bloodstream. The Red Cross tested umbilical cord blood in 2005 and found 21 different pesticides that had crossed the placenta. Additionally, the growth hormones found in non-organic beef and milk are linked with early onset of puberty.

For this reason, experts suggest that mothers eat organically as soon as they know they are pregnant, and continue through the breastfeeding period. Children should eat organically until they are at least 3 years old.

Organic foods are more expensive than the alternative, but you can eat organically on a budget by purchasing organic substitutes for only those foods that contain the worst toxins. These are known as the "dirty dozen." Check out the previous "Yummy Tummy" chapter for more information about the dirty dozen.

Other foods to buy organic include peanut butter, ketchup and baby food. Pesticides used on peanuts are especially toxic. Organic ketchup is actually healthier because it contains 57% more lycopene, which is linked with lower cancer and heart disease risk. It also has double the antioxidants, and less sugar and artificial flavors. For name brand baby food, try Gerber Organic and Earth's Best Organic.

Organic on a budget

There are a few things you can do to save money. First, you don't have to purchase ALL foods organic. Look at the list of the dirty dozen and if

173

you are able to purchase just a few of them in an organic form, you will be doing a lot to limit your intake of pesticides and hormones. Take a good look at your grocery budget and the foods you commonly buy. If there are some foods that you eat all the time that are on the dirty dozen list, then start with those. Read *The Cheaper Organic* for more information.

At about six months, when your baby starts to eat real food, it's a real treat to make your own baby food. Pre-made baby food may be more convenient, but it is cheaper to make your own. When I was a baby, my mother made yummy mashes out of fresh fruits and vegetables. I still remember the flavor of her applesauce, which she continued to make for years. You can make homemade more convenient by placing your baby's food into small containers or ice cube trays, which you just defrost as needed. As always, consult a doctor about your child's dietary requirements.

Breastfeeding

Breastfeeding is awesome in every way. It's free, is better for the baby, adds to the bonding experience, and doesn't impact the environment. But like everything else in our society, retailers have figured out a way to make money off of breastfeeding. Avoid getting sucked into the consumerism of breastfeeding. Make your own or purchase re-usable organic cotton or wool breast pads. Rather than contaminate your nipples, use organic nipple creams, or make your own. Olive oil and lanolin work great.

If you chose to breastfeed, try to detox your body before you give birth to limit the amount of toxins you pass to your baby. This includes eating the most nutritious foods and avoiding chemical based personal care products. See *Beautification, Shopping Organically*, and *The Cheaper Organic* for more information.

If you must bottle feed, try to find fair-trade organic infant formula. It does exist! If you can't find it in stores, try shopping online. Use bottles that do not contain BPA (Bisphenol A), a toxin that leaches out of some plastics. BPA is linked with prostate and breast cancer, weight gain and accelerated puberty.

Shopping Suggestions
- Medela sells not only bottles but also breast pumps that are BPA free.
- Kleankanteen.com - Try Klean Kanteen's stainless steel sippy cup, so you don't have to worry about plastic leaching toxins. Similar products can be found at Target.
- Try glass bottles. Evenflo sells them.
- Use silicone nipples instead of plastic

Resources

Barnes, Lisa. (2005). The Petit Appetit Cookbook: Easy, Organic Recipes to Nurture Your Baby and Toddler

Buck, Angela. (2008). The Everything Organic Cooking for Baby and Toddler Book: 300 naturally delicious recipes to get your child off to a healthy start (Everything Series)

Cox, Jeff. (2008). The Organic Food Shopper's Guide

Grant, Amanda. (2001). Organic Baby and Toddler Foods: The Complete Organic Diet for 0 to 3 Year Olds

Linardakis, Connie and Constantina Linardakis. (2001). Homemade Baby Food Pure and Simple: Your Complete Guide to Preparing Easy, Nutritious, and Delicious Meals for Your Baby and Toddler

Baby Milk Action (www.Babymilkaction.org)

Green People (www.Greenpeople.org/HomeDelivery.html)

International Baby Food Action Network (www.Ibfan.org)

Organic Consumers (www.organicconsumers.org/btc/BuyingGuide.cfm)

Planet Friendly (www.planetfriendly.net/organic.html)

Vegetarian Baby (www.Vegetarianbaby.com) – A site for parents of vegetarian and vegan children under three.

An Eco-Babe Tip:

Homemade Applesauce

Apples
Pressure Canner or Waterbath Canner
Canning jars (I used pint size)
Lids and rings

Wash apples, put about 2 inches of water in a large pot, preferably Stainless Steel, (Aluminum cookware can leach aluminum into the food). Core and cut the apples in wedges, dropping the wedges into the water as you cut each apple. I do not peel my apples as they are organic, if your apples are not organic you will need to peel them because of the pesticides in the peeling. However, organic is best and if you leave the peeling on it just makes the applesauce that much more nutritious.

Make sure the apples dip under the water. If you prefer you can use distilled water to cook the apples. Fill the pot up with apples add water if needed.

Bring to a boil reduce heat to keep from boiling over. Cook until tender. Drain apples, let cool slightly. (My food processor is plastic) Put in food processor and process until the consistency you prefer. Pour into another pot to keep warm, epically if making more.

I do not season my applesauce, however I do have sweet apples. You might try a taste. Once you have all of your applesauce made fill jars and canner according to the canners specifications.
- **Linda Rushing from Smyrna, TN**

Babies in Toyland

I was inspired to write this chapter after I helped a good friend clean out her 5-year-old daughter's toys. That day, we took 6 trashcan bags FULL of toys to the thrift store. Even after we pillaged, her daughter still had mountains of dolls, an entire yard of vehicles, and 3 dressers full of toys. How many toys does one child need? To answer that question, I observed her daughter for three days straight. I discovered that she played with about a dozen toys on a regular basis. These were her favorites, and if someone bought her something new, it was added to the rotation, while something old was ignored. So, do children really need all those toys?

The problem with toy shopping is that you don't know whether or not your child will like the toy enough to play with it more than once. So we keep buying things, hoping to hit the jackpot. Next thing you know, you've spent several hundred dollars on a room full of toys that your child ignores. So when considering a new toy, especially expensive yard toys, try to borrow them first or buy them used. Remember, children don't care if a toy is new or not, they just care if it's fun or not.

It's also important to not get suckered into advertising. I'm talking about movie and television toys. Every time an animated movie or television show comes out, parents are pressured to buy the toys for them. My nephew used to be obsessed with Star Wars, and for several years, he wanted nothing but Star Wars toys. After that, it was Thomas the Train and who knows what it will be next. The problem with these toys is that they're only fun while the show/movie is fun. They are also expensive because you are paying for the name of the show they are advertising. I'm sure my nephew has several hundred dollars worth of Star Wars and Thomas toys that just take up space in his closet. The sad reality is that the average kindergartner knows more logos than presidents, plants and other important things.

Conventional toys (non-organic/fair trade) can also be unsafe for children. Toys made from certain types of plastic like Polyvinyl Chloride (PVC or Vinyl) contain phthalates, which are chemicals known to cause cancer. Phthalates are used to make toys soft, pliable and durable. It's especially dangerous because of the tendency children have to put toys in their mouths. The chemicals are so dangerous that some manufactures no longer use that material in teething toys.

Conventional toys are also known for lead poisoning, toxic paints, and recalls, especially those made in foreign countries. Toys with fabric are often made from non-organic cottons, which mean they contain pesticides. They are also colored with chemical dyes and contain petroleum-based fillers. Even worse are some wooden toys, which are made from wood chips that are glued back together. Not only is the glue toxic, but also the wood is often pine, which emits vapors that can cause allergies and respiratory problems. The potential risks with all of these toys increase significantly when they get scraped, heated (in the car), broken, or otherwise damaged. There is also a risk with battery operated toys, as batteries themselves are made from toxic ingredients.

The alternative is to purchase organic toys. In organic toys, everything from the stuffing to the wood is non-toxic. They are a little more expensive than conventional toys, but remember, you don't need a lot. I know many children who have a single toy trunk filled with toys and they do not suffer for it. Their toys are elegantly crafted and high quality. They last longer and teach children to value and respect their possessions.

We've all known children who purposefully destroy their toys and constantly beg for more. I had a childhood friend like this and she grew up to abuse all her possessions including her car and home. To her, everything was disposable, and she had no pride of ownership or respect for other's possessions. This begins in childhood, so limit your child's toys and let them learn pride and value.

Organic toys won't break your bank. Look beyond name brand organic. Many stores now have their own brand of cheaper organics and the more popular living organically becomes, the cheaper the products will be. Stores like Toys R Us are now increasing the number of organic options not only in toys, but in bedding and skin care as well. You may have to shop around some more, but the end result is that you are providing a safe environment for you child and nothing is more important than that.

Resources

Action for Nature (www.actionfornature.com) – Nonprofit that
    encourages kids to protect the environment
Bringing up baby with safe and green toys
    (http://www.cnn.com/2008/HEALTH/family/12/08/HM.kids.
    going.green/index.html)
Children's Environmental Health Network (www.cehn.org)
Healthy Child, Healthy World (www.healthychild.org)
Planet Green "How to go green: kid's toys"
    (http://planetgreen.discovery.com/go-green/kids-toys/)

So much Stuff!

One thing new parents quickly figure out, is that they didn't need/never use most of those things they purchased and registered for. So many parents get caught up in the excited whirlwind of parenthood, and what better way to celebrate than buy, buy, buy! We buy so many things with that first child, but our intentions are good. We want the best, fastest, safest, most space-agey stuff for our designer babies. Babies have very few needs, so how can you avoid a shopping frenzy?

First, breathe! Before you make any major decisions about your life, take a moment to just breathe and let the idea of parenthood settle in your mind. I know that nine months doesn't seem like a long time, but trust me, it's better to be clearheaded and pregnant, than frazzled and pregnant. Remember the advice to never go clothes shopping or get a new haircut when you're experiencing PMS? Well that same advice works here. So breathe, breathe, breathe.

Furniture Fantasies

Have you ever opened up a Pottery Barn or Crate and Barrel ad and vowed that someday you will have a room just like that? You see the pristine furniture and perfectly coordinated lamps and vases and you just melt. Well, the reality for most people is that they will never have a home like that, either because they can't afford it or because they don't have a live-in maid to maintain it. So before you charge that maple nursery set, it's important to evaluate your needs. A matching crib, changing table and dresser can set you back over $1000.

Your baby will not care or even notice if the furniture in her/his room is brand new, so when it comes to the big-ticket items, think used. You can find great furniture at yard sales, thrift stores and consignment shops for a bargain. You can also check out EBay and Craigslist. However, remember to check recall lists to ensure you are purchasing safe furniture. Make sure that the crib you buy comes with the instructions, as used cribs are more notorious for accidents due to incorrect assembly.

Do your research and if you accidentally buy a crib that is on a recall list, throw it away and do not try to resell it.

Buying used is also good for the environment and your child's health. If you recall in the "Detoxing Your Home" section, new furniture often contains toxic plastics, glues and varnishes. These chemicals give off fumes (Volatile Organic Compounds - VOCs) that can cause asthma, allergies and other respiratory problems. In addition, babies tend to put their mouths on everything, and when they chew or suck on the furniture, they are ingesting those toxins, which in this case are related to cancer and hormonal disorders. If you do have new items, leave them outside for a few days (preferably a month) before bringing them inside. That way the fumes have a chance to wear off. This includes furniture and mattresses.

Take the money you saved on the used furniture and purchase a new organic mattress and organic bedding. Remember; always buy the mattress and car seat new. Studies show that secondhand mattresses are linked with sudden infant death. Used car seats may also have hidden damage that makes them unsafe in an accident. These are also non-toxic and safer for baby. Most major retailers do sell organic bedding and mattresses, and they are not much more expensive than the non-organic options.

Green Furniture

If you do have your heart set on new furniture, or have family members wanting to buy for you, there is another option. Many retailers now sell furniture made of sustainable wood and non-toxic glues and varnishes. These are low in VOCs, which means they do not give off toxic fumes.

So when salespeople and family members try to pressure you to purchase all new furniture, remember what is better for the health of your child and either purchase green or used furniture. If you can't afford organic, buy untreated bedding that is not labeled water resistant or flame retardant, because the chemicals that make them resistant are toxic.

Cut the Clutter – Save Your Budget

A little restraint on your part, and you could save more money in the long term. Many families find that their pre-baby home is too small once they start shopping for the nursery. However, by purchasing less, you might be able to stay in your smaller home and save money on housing costs. It's common for new parents to purchase/rent larger homes when they discover they are pregnant, but this may not be the best option for you. Babies are not cheap, and if you lock yourself into an expensive mortgage or lease, you may find yourself struggling. For most American families, housing, medical and childcare costs consume most of their budget.

Remember, babies don't require much. They need a place to sleep, a way to be carried, a car seat and a high chair. You don't have to go with the traditional either. Some cool space-saving options include organic baby hammocks, space-saving high chairs (look like a car seat with a tray and can be placed anywhere) and co-sleeping (letting your baby sleep in your bed with you). You could also save money by purchasing a convertible crib that will last many years. Skip the changing table. Most parents change their children's diapers at the site of the incident. For diaper storage, a friend of mine just used a shelf on her bookcase. That way the diapers were located where she spent the most time with her baby, her living room.

For carrying baby, I highly suggest slings. They are easy to use, don't strain your back and are comfortable for your passenger. The great thing about slings is that they will last you a while, because they can handle a

★ ★ ★ ★ ★ ★ ★ ★ ★ ★

An Eco-Babe Tip:

The Pack-n-Play is a great buy. For $150 or less, you get a bassinet, crib, and changing table; and it only takes up a two by three foot area (great for small apartments). Plus, it folds up compactly for travel or for easy storage if you want to keep it for your next baby. - **Lisa Pratt, Law Student and Mom to 5 children aged 3 months - 9 years, Springfield, VA**

★ ★ ★ ★ ★ ★ ★ ★ ★ ★

lot of weight. I once carried a tired 4-year-old for two hours while shopping at the mall, without straining my back.

While it's tempting to purchase monitors, mobiles, motorized rockers, and fancy crib toys, you're best checking that need. Ask yourself, "Do I *really* need this? Does my baby *really* need this?" If you think you really do, consider purchasing them secondhand.

What is Your Baby Wearing?

During the first few years of their lives, children outgrow their clothes faster than they outwear them. Because of this, the impact their little clothes have on the world is bigger than yours. If you recall the earlier chapter, "What Are You Wearing?" many name brand retailers manufacture their clothes with sweatshop labor. It's bad enough that your favorite Nike shoes, that you will wear for several years, was made by an abused and underpaid garment worker. It's even worse that the Nike shoes your baby will wear for a month was made by that same garment worker. Children are like those fashion conscious people who refuse to wear an outfit more than once. This is waste at its worst.

Organic fabrics made of hemp, cotton, bamboo and wool are best for a baby's sensitive skin. Not only are organic fabrics more durable, but they also don't contain toxic chemicals.

For eco-conscious parents, buying organic and fair trade may not be enough. Yes, they are pesticide free, but the financial cost and turnaround are not worth it. Secondhand items, even if they are made from conventional cotton, are better because they are cheaper, have already had the pesticides washed out, and are often in great condition. Every time an item is reused, you are reducing its environmental impact. When you compare $.25 to $2 per item at a thrift store to $10 to $30 per item for a new organic item; the cheaper often wins. You could have an entire wardrobe of clothes for your baby for $25 if you buy them secondhand, which leaves more money for more important purchases.

Other Ways to Green Your Baby

Bath and Body

With babies, it's best to keep things as natural and organic and you can. Don't buy into fancy powders, lotions and creams. For a refresher on shopping organically, please re-read the chapters "Beautification" and "Shopping Organically." Continue reading for other cheap, natural and organic options for your little one. For product suggestions, check out the Internet Shopping Guide in the appendices.

Lotion: Believe it or not, plain ol' Olive Oil works best as a lotion on your baby's skin. It's natural, fragrance-free and cheap. To make your olive oil smell better, you can add a few drops of your favorite essential oils. I suggest soothing scents such as lavender, chamomile and sandalwood.

Baby Powder: Talc is actually a toxin, because it can cause damage when inhaled. Try arrowroot powder or cornstarch instead.

Save water by bathing with your baby. It makes for additional bonding time, and is more convenient for mom. This is great for mothers who complain about never having the chance to take a shower because her baby takes up all of her time.

Find more on eco friendly baby creams, lotions, and powders in the shopping guide at the end of the book.

Laundry

When washing babies clothes and diapers, it's best to use organic, natural and fragrance-free soap. Try Dr. Bronner's 18-in-one Castile Soap. For more information, re-read the chapter "Room by Room: The Laundry Room". There you will find information on Maggie's SoapNuts, which are great for washing baby's things.

Decorating

Make sure you use low or no VOC paint in the nursery, to limit the amount of toxic fumes you subject your baby to. I also suggest that you paint at least a month before you expect your baby to arrive, and air out the room, to get rid of any fumes. I don't recommend putting new carpet in the nursery, as carpets not only give of VOCs for a long time; they also trap allergens that can lead to asthma, allergies and other health problems. Consider putting a sustainable wood floor down instead. Check out the "Detoxing Your Home" section for more information.

Attachment parenting and Co-sleeping

Save money on a crib and create a stronger bond with your baby through attachment parenting. Sleeping with your baby not only helps parents bond with their child, it also improves the quality of sleep for everyone. Read The Continuum Concept: In Search Of Happiness Lost by Jean Liedloff.

DIY

With a little craftiness, you can make your own diapers, baby clothes, breast pads and toys.
Check out:
Knitty.com
Ozclothnappies.org
Nappynetwork.com

Sharing Communities

You can find many eco-conscious mother groups on the Internet. While the intent of these groups may be more for networking than swapping used toys, you are guaranteed to find several moms who would love to trade with you. So get out there, get to know mothers in your community, and start swapping. For fun and swapping, have a baby swap party! Every mom brings baby stuff that they no longer need. These things are then placed in a pile in the middle of the room. Once everything is set up, everyone just dives in and takes what they need. Whatever is left over at the end is donated to charity. This is a great way to get rid of stuff you no longer need, get the things you do need, hang out with friends, and donate to charity all in one day!

Elimination Communication

This is a technique to have a diaper-less baby through signals and timing. Yes it is possible! It's best to start before six months of age. Third world and indigenous parents have used Elimination Communication for eons, and it is now making a comeback with eco-conscious parents.

An Eco-Babe Tip:

I started using elimination communication after my fifth baby was born. My three year old, who was already potty trained, began to regress after the baby was born. I desperately did not want to put her back in diapers, so I decided to give EC a try and devised a plan to let the "big sister" help me potty train the baby. Whenever my older daughter used the potty, I would take the baby in there to watch so she could "demonstrate" to the baby how to sit and go potty on the toilet. Every time I changed the baby's diaper, I sat the baby on the potty and her sister would encourage her to go. The baby is now three months old and her big sister is still diligently teaching her how to use the potty. The best part is that once my older daughter had an important role to play in taking care of the baby, her potty regression ended immediately. - **Lisa Pratt, Law Student and Mom to 5 children aged 3 months - 9 years, Springfield, VA**

Resources

Organic Baby (www.Organicbaby.co.nz)
Kids Health (www.Kidshealth.org)
Baby Center (www.Babycenter.com.au)

An Eco-Babe Business Spotlight: A Small Green Footprint

Our Philosophy

Deciding to have a child was a big step for us – as it is for most couples. In addition to the typical topics couples discuss when they talk about having kids, one topic we kept coming back to was the endless consumption that seemed to surround raising children. Two to three (or more) years worth of diapers, plastic at every corner, equipment for every possible task; it just seemed so excessive for our values. Then one day I realized children didn't 'need' all these things to survive and for those things they did need there had to be alternatives to the plastic and the disposables.

Once we made the decision to have kids, I began the search for environmentally friendly products for the baby-to-be. When looking for a product, one might say I would get (and still get) a bit obsessive. I would spend hours searching the internet for the most eco-friendly product out there. I looked at the materials used in the product. Were they natural products such as wood or bamboo or a recycled man-made product such as fleece from soda bottles? Were the paints and finishes non-toxic? What chemicals were used in its production? How was it produced? Was it organically grown and/or sustainable harvested? How far did the finish product have to travel to get to me (gas use, pollution)?

Although I could find products that fit my requirements, I couldn't find all the products I needed on one site. I knew I wasn't the only person out there searching for the safest products for both their children and the environment; but the time required to do all of this product research is prohibitive for many people. So I thought, if I am already doing all of this research for my family, why not create a website with these products that I found. A site where you could be confident that someone had already done the research that you just don't have the time to do, to make sure each of the products you need were eco- and child-friendly. That's what I would have liked; so that is what we have done.

Products

When choosing products we use the following guidelines:

- Products are made from natural materials or from recycled man-made products
- Wood products are sustainably harvested
- Cotton, hemp, and bamboo are naturally grown without pesticides or chemicals.
- Although it is not always possible, we consider the distance a product has to travel to get to us.

In a perfect world, we would choose a product that fits all of these requirements plus be of high quality. When it is not possible, we have chosen what we feel is the best of what is out there. We will update our catalog as we find products that better fit our guidelines. If you know of a product that you feel we should carry, please let us know and we will look into it.

"We do the research so you don't have to"

Environmental Business Practices

In addition to the environmentally-sensitive products we also try to use environmentally-friendly options in other aspects of the business. We use AISO, a socially responsible, green web hosting company that is powered by clean, renewable, solar energy. Whenever possible we reuse boxes and packaging material; when that is not possible we try to use new materials with the highest recycled content. We don't buy Styrofoam peanuts or plastic pillows but we may reuse those that we receive.

For more information, visit **asmallgreenfootprint.com.**
 - Sandy Cederbaum, A Small Green Footprint
"Their feet may grow, but their footprint doesn't have too."

Babes at Work

How Green is your work?

Take this quick yes/no quiz to see how green you work is. To see how much you have improved, take this quiz now and after you have made some positive changes. This allows you to quantify how green you have made your work and keep track of areas for future improvement. Find out what your work's carbon footprint is, **www.carboncounter.**

❑ Do you use CFLS or LED light bulbs?

❑ Are your computers set to automatically go to "sleep" or "hibernate" when they are not in use?

❑ Do you shut down your computers and peripherals at the end of the day?

❑ Do you use both sides of paper?

❑ Do you use recycled stationery?

❑ Do you use recycled office supplies?

❑ Do you use recycled toner cartridges?

❑ Do you reuse envelopes?

❑ Do you reuse shipping boxes?

❑ Do you recycle all of your paper products?

❑ Do you recycle toner cartridges and batteries?

❑ Do you recycle your old computers and electronics?

❑ Do the office cleaners use nontoxic cleaning products?

❑ Do you use nontoxic air fresheners?

❑ Do the sinks have nontoxic alcohol free soap?

❑ Do you use recycled toilet paper and paper towels?

❑ Do employees use reusable cups/water bottles?

❑ Do you encourage no-waste lunches?

❑ Do you have green plants in every room?

❑ Is there adequate ventilation (fresh air) in the building?

❑ Do you purchase fair trade coffee?

❑ Do you encourage car pooling and public transportation?

❑ Do you encourage teleconferencing or telecommuting?

Considering that we spend a quarter of our lives at work, living greener should also include the workplace. If you are the boss and have the power to make changes for a greener workplace – congratulations! If not, you will need to prove to the powers-that-be that a greener workplace is cost effective. A greener workplace not only lessens your environmental impact, it also leads to healthier and more productive employees. Let's start with the many ways your office can save money.

Electricity

Artificial lighting accounts for 44% of the electrical bill in the average office. Energy Star light bulbs and fixtures use two-thirds less energy. So if your electricity costs $300 a month, $132 of that is from lighting alone. Switching to Energy Star lighting will save you $87 a month, which is over $1000 a year. Compact fluorescent (CFL) bulbs are great, and LED lights are even better. You can further your savings by installing timers, dimmers, skylights and motion sensors, and by turning off the lights any time you leave the room for more than a few minutes.

Computers waste electricity amounting to $1 billion dollars a year in the U.S. alone. That is because many people do not shut down their computers at the end of the day. Additionally, people don't set their computers to go to sleep when they are not in use, and if they are turned off, the power strip still sucks electricity. Make it a company policy to have every one turn off their computers at the end of the day, set their computers to go to sleep instead of going to a screensaver, and turn off the power strip. If your IT department schedules backups and other maintenance at night that prevents you from turning off your computer, you can save by setting your computer to go to sleep. This can cut energy use up to 70%. You can save even more energy by investing in Energy Star computers, monitors and printers. If you donate your old computers and peripherals, you may even get a tax break.

Paper

The average office worker in the U.S. uses 10,000 sheets of copy paper every year. You can cut this number in half just by using both sides of the paper. I used to temp at an office, where paper that was printed one sided was marked with an "X" and then added back to the printer. Once the paper was printed on both sides, it was shredded and then recycled. The company would also use paper that was printed one sided to make a version of post-its. The paper was cut into eighths and stapled together. They saved hundreds of dollars a year by not having to buy post-its.

In addition, avoid color printing and print in draft mode when you can. Switch to chlorine-free and recycled paper. Recycled paper uses half the water to produce than regular paper. It also takes 70% less energy to make recycled paper. You might try alternative paper made from bamboo, hemp, kenaf, or organic cotton. You can also get envelopes, files, folders and other paper products with post-consumer content. Make sure your office recycles its toner and ink cartridges. Most manufacturers provide a way for you to return them for free. Manufacturers then use the recycled cartridges to make remanufactured ones. Each remanufactured cartridge saves 2.5 pounds of metal and plastic and a half-gallon of oil.

Make recycling paper easier by limiting the amount you have to deal with. When your business get junk mail, be it mailers, unwanted catalogs or newsletters, contact the distributors and ask to be removed from the mailing list. You should be able to remove yourself from any advertising you receive in the mail; otherwise it's illegal. Also check to see if any of your wanted magazines, catalogs, or newsletters are available in an electronic format. That way you can just store it on your computer, instead of receiving a printed copy. If possible, have your office sign up for electronic billing, and store statements on the computer, rather than in print.

If you have a network, where employees can share files, make sure you put all employee manuals, phone lists, instruction manuals, and forms on there. That way you don't have to distribute paper copies. Use electronic paperwork and store files on the computer whenever you can. Check out Greenprint software, which eliminates blank pages from documents before you print them. It also allows you to convert files to PDF for paperless document sharing.

Office Supplies

Try to shop for recycled and reusable products for your office supplies. Try refillable pens made from sustainable materials and pencils made from recycled materials. Reuse envelopes that you receive in the mail for interoffice use. Tape a sheet of lined paper to them, and set columns for "To" and "From. When I worked at Northern Arizona University, my department never had to buy our own manila envelopes. You can also find binders, folders, and other office supplies made from recycled and recyclable materials. Look for the chasing arrows symbol.

Need help finding green office products? Just look for these certifications and seals of approval.

Green Seal – Products with this certification are environmentally preferred based on its creation, ingredients, use and recyclability (cradle-to-grave). Visit greenseal.org for more information.

FSC – The Forest Stewardship Council ensures wood products come from responsibly managed forests. This includes paper products. Visit fsc.org for more information.

Energy Star – The Energy Star certification is given only to electronics that use energy efficiently and have reduced use "sleep" or "standby" modes. Visit Energystar.gov for more information.

WaterSense – For water efficient products look for the WaterSense label of the Environmental Protection Agency. www.epa.gov/watersense

Fair Trade – You can guarantee you are buying Fair Trade when you see the Fair Trade seal of the Fair Trade Labeling Organizations International. Visit fairtrade.net for more information.

Green Globe – For green travel resources look for the Green Globe certification. This certification is for hotels, restaurants, resorts and car rental agencies. Visit greenglobe.org for more information.

Organic – For food and cleaning products look for the USDA (United States Department of Agriculture) organic certification. www.ams.usda.gov/nop

The Dress Code

Have a dress code that reflects your green values. Order uniforms from fair trade businesses. If you use a laundry service, make sure you work with one that uses ecofriendly products and practices. You can even offer employees a uniform allowance for wearing fair trade and organic clothes to work. A more casual dress code can save you on air conditioning costs as well, as formal clothes make employees feel hotter. Every degree you can raise on your air conditioning thermostat saves you up to 20% on AC costs.

Recycling

Just about everything in an office can be recycled, from paper to PDAs. Make it a company policy to recycle and purchase recycled office supplies. Place recycling bins throughout the office and create a company manual for recycling. You could even make recycling a competition, and the division/department that recycles the most wins a pizza party. Check out the "Recycling" chapter.

Have an eco-leader or eco-team at work whose job is to ensure that green values are expressed in all areas of the business and decision-making. They could even be in charge of competitions and running a green-suggestion box. If you think your business is a green leader, check out epa.gov/climateleaders. This program allows you to network with other industry leaders, share green knowledge and receive recognition for your performance.

The Break Room

Stop purchasing disposable plates and utensils for your break room. Instead, make a one-time purchase of reusable cups, dishes and utensils. Provide organic dish soap to encourage employees to clean their own dishes. If you have to, put up a little sign reminding them that their mother doesn't work there!

If your office provides food or drinks (coffee, tea, and creamer) in the break room, switch to Fair Trade, organic and local items. This goes for office parties and events as well. It's also great if the office has filtered drinking water, to reduce bottled-water use.

If your co-workers often order take-out, try to combine your orders to limit the amount of packaging waste. If your co-workers often leave the office to eat out, encourage them to bike or walk to the restaurant, instead of driving. You could even set up a reward system for employees who exercise (walk/bike to restaurant) on their lunch breaks.

Your office can also switch to nontoxic cleaning products and recycled paper or cloth towels in the bathrooms and kitchen. Try to buy all office and cleaning supplies in bulk to limit the amount of packaging waste. Reuse the shipping boxes.

The Office Environment

With the wide array of chemicals floating around the average office, it's important to do what you can to limit them. Cleaning supplies often contain harsh chemicals and scents. This can lead to allergies, asthma, frequent headaches, and other health problems. Switching to nontoxic and biodegradable cleaning supplies may make an impact on the amount of sick days the staff need.

Indoor plants are not only pleasing to the eye; they also help to absorb indoor pollution. Opt for plants that don't have a strong scent, like Ferns, Ficuses, and Succulents. Install ceiling fans to circulate air.

Furniture and carpeting can give off volatile organic compounds (VOCs) that are related to many health problems including birth defects and cancer. Most offices won't be able to redecorate, but you can change their policy for future purchases. For all future purchases, look for furniture, carpeting and paint that is free of VOCs. With wooden furniture, shop for products made from sustainable materials with a nontoxic finish. Avoid furniture made from particleboard or fake wood, as it is usually made from wood dust and toxic glue. Check out Herman-Miller and Steelcase, who have a groundbreaking line of eco-friendly office furniture. Look for Greenguard certified furniture. Greenguard is a non-profit organization whose goal is to find and certify products that will help maintain healthy interior air in offices.

If your place of employment is being built, consider installing a vegetated or green roof[56]. This is basically, a roof covered in grass or a similar ground cover. This improves thermal insulation and helps manage rainwater runoff. Green roofs save money on heating and cooling, and last longer than traditional roofs. If you have a decent budget, plant a roof garden. This would be a great place for guests and/or employees to lounge.

Finally, sunlight and fresh air are free and do wonders not only for the office environment, but also for employee health and productivity. Open those windows! Read "Detoxing Your Home" for even more ideas on how to have a green and healthy workplace.

Telecommuting

If you can work from home give it a try. With all the great technology available today, many office tasks can be easily accomplished from home. Telecommuting is great for the environment because it means one less car on the road. It's also better for employees because if there are any emergencies at home, they are right there. Parents with sick children won't have to miss a day of work. 44 million Americans have telecommuting jobs.

If you can't telecommute, consider a consolidated workweek. You would work four ten-hour shifts instead of five eight –hour shifts. This allows employees to drive one less day to work, and gives them three-day weekends. This helps increase productivity.

Rather than travel by air or car, have virtual meetings or teleconferences. These can be easily accomplished with conference calls and chat software.

LEED

If your office has the means and the desire, they can also make renovations to the building to save money, and make a huge positive impact on the environment. Consider getting LEED certified. This is a certification for the greenest of green buildings. It's a mark of distinction and respect. Look into solar power, solar hot water heaters, low-flow and waterless toilets, rainwater collection, grey water recycling, and grass roofs. LEED certification is also rewarded by tax breaks and credits in many areas.

Investments and Networking

If you offer your employees a retirement investment plan, make sure you have green options that allow them to invest their retirement funds in sustainable businesses, industries, and green power sources.

Create partnerships with green community groups through donations and volunteering. This can improve your reputation as well as customer loyalty. You can even set up a workplace charitable giving program.

Network with other green businesses to share knowledge. If your workplace is involved in a lot of business-to-business transactions, make sure you are purchasing your goods from green and local businesses.

Publicly report your business environmental efforts and progress. This can enhance your reputation and give you a way to quantify your performance (Globalreporting.org). You can calculate your business carbon footprint at ghgprotocol.org.

Resources

Charity Navigator (www.charitynavigator.org) – Guide to donating to
  nonprofits.
General Electric Credit Card (www.myearthrewards.com) – A credit
  card that gives you carbon offsets as a reward.
Social Investment Forum (www.socialinvest.org) – Gives you
  information on how to invest your money in a socially responsible
  way.

The Commute

The average American spends 47 hours a year in rush hour traffic. That's a lot of gas wasted in traffic. If you drive to work, there are several things you can do to save gas, and therefore lessen your environmental impact.

1. Tighten your gas cap – Every year 147 MILLION gallons of gas evaporate because of loose gas caps.
2. Fill your tires frequently – Under inflated tires waste 2-3 mpg, because the car uses more energy to rotate them.
3. Change your air filter every 6 months – A dirty engine has to work harder, which means it uses more gas. So don't choke it with a dirty air filter.
4. Find the cheapest gas – This doesn't save the planet, but it does help our checkbooks. Go to gasbuddy.com or gaspricewatch.com to find the cheapest gas in your city. Use the money you save to buy organic.
5. Drive a little slower, don't rev your engine, and don't accelerate too fast – The faster and harder you drive, the more gas you waste. For example to go from driving 75 to 62mph, improves gas consumption by 15%.
6. Consider trading in your gas-guzzler for a gas efficient car.
7. Consider joining a car-sharing service like Zipcar instead of owning your own car. (zipcar.com)
8. Carpooling, bicycling and public transportation are the most efficient ways to get to work. If every car in America carried one more passenger, we would save 8 billion gallons of gas. – Try an electric bike!
9. If your business has a fleet, make sure the cars are green. Visit greenfleets.org and fueleconomy.gov.

Alternative Fuels

Most alternative fuels are a quick fix and are in no way a substitute for oil. They require land, water, and food. I appreciate the fact that scientists are trying to come up with alternatives to oil, but the reality is that using corn or sugarcane as a fuel is just as dangerous for the environment and our society as oil based fuel. Using a crop for fuel is dangerous because of the toxic chemicals used to grow the crop and the massive amount of water that is used/irrigated/polluted. Until scientists figure out a way to use trash as a fuel, the best thing we can do is conserve. That said, here is a quick rundown of alternative fuels.

Ethanol – This is made mostly out of corn and sugarcane. In the United States, we don't use pure ethanol. It is mixed with regular gas. It pollutes less than gas, but gives you less mileage, so it is used as an additive.

Cellulosic ethanol – This is similar to regular ethanol except it is made from agricultural waste and wood chips. This is a lot better because it doesn't require food crops. This one is still in the works, but I suspect we will see more of it in the future.

Biodiesel – This is made mostly from soybeans, another food crop, however, some ingenious people have figured out how to make it out of grease and fat. Grease is a byproduct of our fast food culture and we produce three billion gallons of it a year. If you have a car that currently runs on diesel #2, you can convert to biodiesel. I highly, highly recommend it because conventional diesel is a big polluter. Check out www.biodiesel.org for more information.

Bioethanol – This is made with grains, much like alcohol. Just like ethanol, it requires a food crop to work and can run in regular gas engines. The problem with it is that it is corrosive, which means it would damage our pipeline, so at this point it is not viable as a mainstream fuel.

Liquid Petroleum Gas, LPG – This is basically propane. It is in use currently. Many buses and fleet vehicles run on it. It runs cleaner than gasoline, but has storage requirements that do not make it viable for the average car. The tank is large and heavy.

Hybrid – This is a combination of gasoline and electricity. When you drive slow and mellow, you are running on electricity. When you rev your engine, or speed up to pass someone, the car kicks in with the gas. If you want to get more technical, Google it. ☺

Personally, I'm not too impressed with hybrids thus far. Ten years ago, you could buy a car that got 30 miles to the gallon and that was just the norm. Now all of a sudden auto manufacturers are gushing about hybrids that can get 25-40 miles to a gallon. Maybe I'm demanding too much from them, but when my 1994 Mercury Tracer can get 40 miles to a gallon, just by driving mellow and maintaining it, is it too much to ask for a hybrid that could get 60-80 miles to a gallon??? And what is up with the hybrid SUVs and trucks? I think it's just a marketing ploy to keep people buying cars bigger than they need. So, celebrities can keep their pretty Prius', and I will hold out for something better. If you do own a Prius or hybrid, I applaud you for thinking about the environment when making such an important purchase. It was also a good investment, as they will probably have a good trade-in value for when auto manufactures make a better one.

Electric Cars – I can't wait until someone starts selling electric cars again. Did you know we already had a viable electric car on the market several years ago? In fact the electric car was invented in the 1800s! In the 1990s GM released the EV1, but it didn't last. There is a conspiracy behind that car, because even though they worked beautifully, the company took them back from everyone and destroyed them. If you want to learn more about it, watch the movie "Who Killed the Electric Car?" There are several green celebrities interviewed in the film, who had their green cars taken from them (Mel Gibson, Tom Hanks, Alexandra Paul, Peter Horton, Ed Begley, Jr.). It's highly enjoyable and might just frustrate you into activism! Check out www.sonyclassics.com/whokilledtheelectriccar for more information.

Electric cars would run completely on electricity. This means that they would end our dependence on oil and significantly reduce our carbon emissions. Electric cars don't pollute, however the parts required to make it work do. We still need to invent a battery that isn't lead acid based. It's a better option than gasoline based vehicles, but it still has its downsides.

Hydrogen – These cars would run on hydrogen requiring either natural gas or water. It's a great concept, however to get it to work requires a large amount of power. So it's not really feasible right now. The problem with hydrogen cars is that they still produce carbon monoxide emissions just like gasoline cars.

Solar Powered Cars – This is in the works. The car would be covered in Photovoltaic cells that would convert solar energy into electricity. Scientists are trying two different ways to get this to work. One way is the have the car completely powered by solar energy. The other way is to use the solar energy in tandem with fuel, like a hybrid car. This science is still a few years away as we still need to make the photo cells more efficient. Currently we can only convert 15% of the sun's energy.

Blue-green algae – If we can get this to work, it would be wonderful. The car would run off of the oil that can be harvested from the algae. What is great about this is that algae require carbon dioxide to grow, so it would eat the fumes and emissions and clean our air.

To learn about other alternative fuels in the works, check out **www.futurecars.com/future_fuels.html**.

Appendices

Appendices

Tear Out Beauty Shopping Tips

Here are some quick tips to remember:

Not tested on animals – While the finished product may not have been tested on animals, this doesn't mean that the individual ingredients weren't tested on animals. So make sure you look for other organic clues before you purchase. Keep Shopping.

Natural, hypoallergenic – These terms mean absolutely nothing. Keep shopping.

Organic –Keep a look out for the "USDA Organic" seal, a statement of certification from the California Organic Farmers Association (COFA), or "100% Organic" from a reliable state or local body. In order to be certified organic, a product must contain at least 70% organic ingredients, not counting the water. If you are unsure about a product, move on.

Avoid certain unpronounceable ingredients–Here is a partial list of some ingredients to avoid, based on information from www.beautytruth.net.

☹ <u>**Methyl, Propyl, Butyl and Ethyl Parabens**</u> –They can be found in almost all non-organic hair and skin products.

☹ <u>**Coal Tar**</u> – This is found in most dandruff shampoos, anti-itch creams, and some synthetic colors.

☹ <u>**Sodium Lauryl Sulfate and Sodium Laureth Sulfate (SLS)**</u>

☹ <u>**Hydroquinone**</u> – This is found in facial lotions and skin lighteners.

☹ <u>**Formaldehydes also known as: DMDM hydantoin, Quaternium 15, Diazolidinyl Urea, Imidazolidinyl Urea, 2-bromo-2-nitropropane-1, 3-diol**</u>

Appendices

☹ **Synthetic Colors labeled as FD&C or D&C, followed by a color and a number**

☹ **Synthetic Fragrances often labeled simply as "fragrance"-**

☹ **Parraffin (mineral oil, petroleum)** – It's ironically found in chap sticks, lip balm, lip stick, and lotions among other personal care products.

☹ **Triclosan** – This is found in most antibacterial products, as well as toothpaste and makeup.

☹ **Alcohol, isopropyl (SD-40)** –This can be found in many products from hair spray and perfume, to antibacterial hand wash and antifreeze. One ounce is considered a FATAL dose.

☹ **Aluminum** –You will find it in most personal care products, like eye shadow, hair dye, and antiperspirants.

☹ **Lead and Mercury (lead acetate and thimerosol)**– It is found in toothpaste and men's hair dye.

☹ **Mainstream Sunscreen with the following ingredients: Octyl-Dimethyl-Para-Amino-Benzoic Acid and Oxybenzone** – These are ironically linked with skin cancer. A better alternative is a sunscreen with Titanium Dioxide in it.

☹ **p-Phenylenediamine (1,4-Benzenediamine, p-Phenyldiamine, 4-Phenylenediamine)**– This is found in most do-it-yourself hair dyes.

☹ Others to watch out for: Polyethylene Glycol (PEG), Talc, Acrylates, Methacrylates, Tocopherol Acetate, anything with the word 'paraben' in it,benzalkonium chloride, cetrimonium bromide, quaternium-15, quaternium 1-29, anything with the world 'chloride' in it, benzyl alcohol, carbomers, dimethicone, dimethicone copolyol, cyclomethicone.

A Letter From Stephanie: Buy Nothing Christmas

Dear Family and Friends,

I love you all, but I've had it. This can't happen again this year. I must speak up. I'm talking about the consumerism of the winter season. I don't care what religion you subscribe to, but what the holidays have become goes against everything positive in EVERY religion. Did Moses say, "Let my people go! Oh and don't forget to buy me another lame sweater and pack of socks this winter!" ☺

NO!

Why is it, that no matter how poor we are, we always dig a little deeper in debt just to paste fake smiles on our faces as we pass a 'symbol of love wrapped in a bow' to relatives we've seen maybe once during the year? Does it really mean we love each other when we exchange scented candles and jewelry? How about the children; what are we teaching them? Winter used to be a time of reflection and bonding; where we bundle together and rest from a year of hard work, and contemplate on the adventures that spring will bring. The season, regardless if it's Christmas, Kwanzaa, Yule, or Chanukah, is about cherishing our family and being thankful that we survived another year.

Yes, I know you love me too, but why do you feel like you're a bad person if you don't buy me something? Why do you feel guilty?

But you say, "Oh, what about the children? I have to buy them something! It just won't be Christmas without presents! I grew up with presents and I want my children to experience that too!"

Will it BE Christmas if your electricity is shut off or you can't afford to put gas in the car to drive to work? Do your children really need more hot wheels, dolls and little parts that you will just slowly throw away over the course of the coming year? Will your children REALLY stop loving you if don't give them STUFF, but instead give them

207

MEMORIES?

How many memories do you have of the holidays? If you're like me, most of them revolve around funny and/or tragic things that happened, rather than the gifts themselves. I remember going to grandma's house and the first thing my sister and I would do, would be to sit and play (horribly) with the piano in the den. I also remember hanging out with the girls across the street and spinning underneath the willow trees in the front yard. Remember the year Dad actually wore the Santa Hat? Do I remember the presents? No. I remember the experiences with my family.

So instead of charging it, PLEASE, PLEASE think seriously about what you are doing. Let's build on old family traditions and start new ones. Instead of exchanging presents, what if we got down and dirty with some Elmer's and glitter to make ornaments for each other, or played a silly board game, or went to the park to play a game of men vs. women football! (Yes that means you too Nana!) There are so many great things we can do, other than exchange gifts.

Last year, when I gave my nephew a foosball table and he said, "I didn't ask for this, I don't want it," it was a slap in the face. My first feelings were of hurt and rejection. After that washed over me, I realized that I felt like he loved me less, which was stupid. I was allowing a THING to quantify love. Now that Christmas memory is tainted by the memory of rejection over a stupid $40 foosball table that collects dust. I was short on the electric bill to buy that for them. I also now realize that by perpetuating this gift exchange in substitution for love, that we are creating jerks. Yes I said it! All of our holidays are earmarked by gift exchanges, which teach our children that love can be quantified. Think about it. A diamond engagement ring means he loves you more than a cubic zirconium ring. Roses and chocolate means she/he loves you more. Sexy lingerie means she loves you more. A better iPod, a fancier car, a cooler snowboard, a faster computer, a sexier dress…all these things mean that someone loves you more.

In a global economy that is stifling and on its way to a recession, is it really wise to teach our children that money equals love? That is what we do every winter.

So I challenge you to buy NOTHING this Christmas, Kwanzaa, Yule, Chanukah, New Years, Valentines Day, etc. You could even try a buy nothing YEAR! Create memories and have fun doing it.

If you have some questions about this concept or need some ideas on how to have a buy nothing holiday, check out www.buynothingchristmas.org and www.newdream.org/commerc/100holiday.html. Buynothingchristmas.org is a Christian Mennonite website. A Canadian group runs it, but it is not limited to them. It's a concept that is good for all people and all beliefs.

Love,
Stephanie

Internet Shopping Guide

To support women-owned businesses, search these first! - Hyena Cart (www.HyenaCart.com) & WAHM (www.WAHMmall.com)

Menstrual Products
- Diva Cup (www.Divacup.com)
- Glad rags (www.Gladrags.com)
- Goddess pads (www.Goddesspads.com)
- Luna pads (www.Lunapads.com)
- Moon pads (www.Moodpads.com)
- Pandora Pads (www.Pandorapads.com)
- Sckoon (www.Sckoon.com)
- The Keeper (www.Thekeeper.com)
- Yoni (www.Yoni.com)

Sewing Instructions to make your own
- Adahy's Cloth Pad Patterns (http://shewhorunsintheforest.googlepages.com)
- Fuz Baby (www.fuzbaby.com/articles/makeyourown_clothm enstrualpads)
- Jan Andrea (www.sleepingbaby.net/jan/Baby/PADS.html)
- Many Moons Alternatives (www.manymoonsalternatives.com)
- Tiny Birds Organics (www.tinybirdsorganics.com/organiccotton/clothp ads)
- WikiHow (www.wikihow.com/Make-Your-Own-Reusable-Menstrual-Pads)
- Women's Environmental Network (WEN) (www.wen.org.uk/sanpro/reports/makeyourown_ web.pdf)

Personal-Care Products

*Approved by organicconsumers.org.

- *Dr. Bronner's (www.drbronner) - 100% USDA organic, animal friendly, and Fair Trade. Their castile soap has 18 uses. You can use if from body soap, toothpaste, shampoo, to counter cleaner and laundry soap! It's all safe.
- *Grateful Body (www.gratefulbody.com) - Also sells a line of products for mature women.
- *Organic Essence (www.organic-essence.com) - This is one of the few companies we know where the entire product line is USDA Organic.
- *Sensibility Soaps (www.sensibilitysoaps.com)
- *Terressentials (www.terressentials)
- *Trillium Organics (www.trilliumorganics.com)
- *Vermont Soap (www.vermontsoap.com)
- Aubrey Organics (www.aubrey-organics.com)
- Avalon Organics (www.avalonorganics.com)
- Bubble and Bee (www.bubbleandbee.com) – Try their Pit Putty Deodorant. It's my favorite.
- Dr. Hauschka (www.drhauschka.com) – This company was voted one of the "Top Brands with a Conscience" in 2006.
- Erbaviva (www.erbaviva.com)
- Ikove by Florestas (www.ikove.com)
- Inky Loves Nature (www.inkylovesnature.com) – Vegan certified and geared toward women of color.
- Jason (www.jason-natural.com)
- Juice Beauty (www.juicebeauty.com) – Some products are certified USDA organic; some are certified by a different authority.
- Kiss my Face (www.kissmyface.com)

- Kuumba Made (www.kuumbamade.com) – This company makes it's products by hand. Also sells fragrances. Some products are 80+% certified organic by
- Making Cosmetics (www.Makingcosmetics.com) - For kits to make your own makeup!
- Natures Gate (www.natures-gate.com)
- Organic Apoteke (www.organicapoteke.com) – Higher end products.
- Pangea Organics (www.pangeaorganics.com) – Certified organic by a different authority than the USDA.
- Pharmacopia (www.pharmacopia.net)
- Poof's Closet (www.poofscloset.com)
- Savage Beauty (www.savagebeauty.net)
- Suki (www.sukisnaturals.com) – Higher end than other brands.
- Weleda (www.usa.weleda)

Hair Products

- Eco Bella (www.ecobella.com)
- Eco Colors (www.ecocolors.net)
- John Masters (www.johnmasters.com)
- Kiss my face (www.kissmyface.com)
- Max Green Alchemy (www.maxgreenalchemy.com) – Vegan.
- Modern Organic Products (www.moporganics.com)
- Surya (www.bodyofgrace.com)
- The Henna Company (www.bytheplanet.com)
- Tints of Nature (www.tintsofnatureusa.com) – Hair dye.
- Tourmaline Ionic Hair Dryer (www.folica.com)

Dental Hygiene

- Eco Friendly toothbrush for kids (www.eco-dent.com) - It has a replaceable head.

- Preserve Toothbrush (www.recycline.com) - Want to recycle your toothbrush? Preserve Toothbrush sells a toothbrush that when you're done with it, you can send it back to them and they recycle them into furniture.

Toothpaste

- Coral White (www.coralcalcium.com)
- Dr. Bronner's (www.drbronners.com) – You can use the castile soap (in small amounts) to brush your teeth. Their castile soap has 18 uses.
- Kiss My Face (www.kissmyface.com)
- Tom's of Maine (www.tomsofmaine.com)
- White Glo (www.greatwhitetrading.com)

Cosmetics

- After Glow Cosmetics (www.afterglowcosmetics.com)
- Aubrey Organics (www.aubrey-organics.com)
- Cargo (www.sephora.com)
- Ecobella (www.ecobella.com)
- Emani Minerals (www.emani.com)
- Gabriel Cosmetics (www.gabrielcosmetics.com)
- Jane Iredale (www.janeiredale.com
- Lavera (www.lavera.com)
- Mineral Fusion (www.mineralfusioncosmetics.com)
- Nvey Eco (www.econveybeauty.com)
- PeaceKeeper Cause-Metics (www.iamapeacekeeper) - PeaceKeeper Cause-Metics is the first cosmetic line to give all of its after tax distributable profits to Women's Health Advocacy and Human Rights issues.
- Susan Posnick (www.susanposnick.com)

Fragrance

- Aubrey Organics (www.aubrey-organics.com)
- Hood River Lavender (www.lavenderfarms.net)
- Jo Anne Bassett (www.joannebassett.com)
- Kate's Magik (www.katesmagik.com)
- Patyka Perfume (www.puresha.com)
- Wyndmere (www.wyndmere.com)

Nail Polish

- Honey Bee Gardens (www.honeybeegardens.com) – Their peel-off polish is great for kids.
- No Miss (www.nomiss.com)
- PeaceKeeper Cause-Metics (www.iamapeacekeeper)
- Priti (www.abeautifullife.com) – Soy and corn based polish.
- SpaRitual (www.sparitual.com)
- Zoya (www.zoya) – Higher end products.

Organic Clothing

- American Apparel (www.americanapparel.net)
- Blue Canoe (www.bluecanoe.com)
- Del Forte (www.greenloop.com) – Organic Jeans.
- Earthpak (www.earthpak.com) - Backpacks and bags.
- Eco Goods (www.ecogoods.com) - Socks, sandals and jeans.
- Hemp Sisters (www.hemp) – Beanies, scarves, and gloves.
- I Wood Design (www.iwooddesign.com) – Sunglasses.
- Lapsaky organic clothing (www.lapsaky.com)
- Loomstate (www.loomstate.org) – Great casual wear.
- Maggie's Functional Organics (www.maggiesorganics.com)
- Nau (www.nau.com) – Casual, office, and trendy clothes.
- No Sweat Apparel (www.nosweatapparel.com) – Boots, work clothes, pants and tees.
- Patagonia (www.patagonia.com) – Sports and casual wear.

- PM Organics (www.pmorganics.com) – Textiles You Feel Good About!
- Prairie Underground (www.prairieunderground.com) – Trendy and Funky.
- Raw Earth Wind Sky (www.rawearthwindsky.com
- Rawganique (www.rawganique.com) – Organic Hemp Clothes.
- Sweat Free (www.sweatfree.org)
- Sworn Virgins (www.hoopladc.com) – Bamboo dresses.
- The Gaiam catalog (www.gaiam)
- The Grain Collective (www.thegraincollective.com) – Check out the bamboo shirts.
- Tonic Shirts (www.tonicshirts.com)
- Under the Canopy (www.underthecanopy.com) – Underwear, bed linens, bathrobes.
- Undesigned (www.undesigned.com) - Trendy clothes.
- Water Girl (www.watergirlusa.com) – Sportswear and swimwear.

Shoes

- Blackspot Sneakers (www.adbusters.org/campaigns/blackspot)
- Charmone (www.charmone.com)
- Moo Shoes (www.mooshoes.com)
- Simple's Eco-Sneak (www.simpleshoes.com)
- Terraplana (www.terraplana.com)

Jewelry - *Made from conflict-free diamonds, recycled silver and gold, and/or fair trade.*

- Brian Bentley (www.porterhousecrafts.com)
- Brilliant Earth (www.brilliantearth.com)
- Earthwise Jewelry (www.leberjeweler.com)
- Fiema (www.fiema.com)

Appendices

- Great Green Goods (www.greatgreengoods.com)
- Green Karat (www.greenkarat.com)
- Harriete Estel Berman (www.harriete-estel-berman.info/jewelry/jewel.html) – Higher end.
- Jennifer Northrup (www.zanisa.com)
- Kirsten Muenster (www.kirstenmuenster.com)
- Maize Hutton (www.maizehutton.com)
- Moonrise (www.moonrisejewelry.com)

Babes At Home

Green Cleaning

- **An Eco-Babe Business:** To me, green is more than just a color it is a way of life. I have been working with essential oils and herbs for the past 15 years. I am an educator, environmentalist and entrepreneur with two successful brands on the market. GreenTerpene.com and eoilco.com. – **Rachel Markel, College Professor-Miami Dade College, University Of Miami and Barry University. Miami, Florida.**
- **An Eco-Babe Business:** Veriuni Earth sells family-safe cleaning products that are both effective and economical. I use the products and have been really impressed. I especially like the Basin, Tub and Tile cleanser. It has brought up some stains that were in our bathroom when we bought our house. I also, really like the Stain Treatment. Go to: tinyurl.com/3mtfa6 – **Linda Rushing, Sales Rep, Smyrna, TN**
- Art Home (www.fruits-passion.com) - Cleaning products by Fruits of Passion.
- B_E_E Cleaning Products (www.bee.net.nz/products.html)
- Biokleen (www.biokleenhome.com)

216

- Cellulose Kitchen Sponges – you can find these on Amazon.com and Target.com
- Citra-Solv (www.citra-solv.com) – Makes a great dishwasher detergent.
- Citrus Magic 5 in1 (www.citrusmagic.com) – This is a really strong cleaner.
- Clean George Hand Sanitizer (www.cleangeorge.com) – A great alcohol free hand sanitizer.
- Earth Friendly Products (www.ecos.com)
- E-Cloth - microfiber cleaning towels and mops (www.enviroproducts.co.uk/)
- Eco Concepts (www.ecoconceptsusa.com)
- Ecover (www.ecover) – Makes a great dishwasher detergent and antibacterial alternatives.
- Imus's Greening the Cleaning (www.imusranchfoods.com) - All profits benefit Imus Cattle Ranch for Kids with Cancer.
- Maggie's Soap Nuts (www.maggiespureland.com)
- Method (www.methodhome.com) – You can find this brand at Target.
- Microfiber cloths for dusting, cleaning, and drying – you can find these on amazon.com
- Mrs. Meyers (www.mrsmeyers.com)
- No Wet (www.nowet.com) - Waterless car wash system
- Orange Glo (www.greatcleaners.net)
- Orange Guard (www.orangeguard.com) – Pest Control
- Planet (www.planetinc.com)
- Seventh Generation (www.seventhgeneration.com) – I love the toilet bowl cleaner!
- Sun and Earth (www.sunandearth.com)
- Swheat Scoop (www.swheatscoop.com) - Biodegradable kitty litter.

Paper Products

- 365 Everyday Value Toilet Paper, Paper Towels, Napkins (www.wholefoodsmarket)
- Ambiance Toilet Paper by Atlantic Packaging
- April Soft Toilet Paper by Atlantic Packaging
- Atlantic Paper Towels (www.atlanticpaper.com/index2.html)
- Bella Napkins (www.marcalpaper.com)
- Best Value Toilet Paper, Paper Towels (www.cascades.com/_home)
- Earth First Toilet Paper, Paper Towels, Napkins (www.royalpaper.us/earth_first.php)
- Fiesta Paper Towels, Toilet Paper by Atlantic Packaging
- Fluff Out Facial Tissue (www.marcalpaper.com)
- Green Forest Toilet Paper, Facial Tissue, Paper Towels, Napkins (www.greenforest-products.com)
- Hankies Facial Tissue (www.marcalpaper.com)
- Marcal Facial Tissue, Napkins, Toilet Paper, Paper Towels (www.marcalpaper.com)
- Pert Paper Towels, Toilet Paper (www.cascades.com/_home)
- Planet Toilet Paper, Paper Towels (www.planetinc.com)
- Seventh Generation Toilet Paper, Paper Towels, Facial Tissue, Napkins (www.seventhgeneration.com)
- Sofpac Toilet Paper (www.marcalpaper.com)

Furniture

- A Natural Home (www.anaturalhome.com)
- Abundant Earth (www.abundantearth.com)
- Anna Sova (www.annasova.com) - Organic Towels
- EcoBedroom (www.ecobedroom.com)
- EcoChoices (www.ecochoices.com)
- Gaiam (www.gaiam) – Organic towels and linens.
- Greenfeet (www.greenfeet.com)

- IF Green (www.ifgreen.com)
- Nirvana Safe Haven (www.nontoxic) – For great organic, wool comforters.
- Savvy Rest (www.savvyrest.com)
- Serenity Pillows (www.serenitypillows.com)
- Shepherd's Dream (www.shepherdsdream.com) – Wool Mattresses
- Tamalpais (www.tamalpais.com)
- The Organic Mattress Store (www.theorganicmattressstore.com)
- Tilonia (www.tilonia.com)
- Under the Canopy (www.underthecanopy.com)
- White Lotus (www.whitelotus.net)
- Whole Foods ECO Lifestyle Stores (www.wholefoodsmarket)

Green Home

- **An Eco-Babe Business:** Do you ever wish you had a personal assistant who knew the birthdays of all your friends and family and was ready to mail out your customized cards on time for every holiday and occasion? Now you can with our unique internet-based system (and these are NOT e-cards). Visit GreetingsByChristine.com today to learn more and to receive your FREE gift account. – **Christine Dew, Business Owner, Surprise, AZ.**
- Blue Wick Candles (www.Bluewick.com)
- Caroma water saving toilets (www.Caromausa.com/toilets)
- Cet Solar (www.cetsolar.com) – Toilet supplies
- Earthwise Bags (www.Earthwisebags.com)
- Eco Bags (www.Ecobags.com)
- Envirolet composting Toilets (www.Envirolet.com)
- Green Earth Office Supply PVC-Free cellophane wrap (www.greenearthofficesupply.com)

- Green Pan Non-Toxic Cookware (www.Green-pan.com/dev/ae/html/products.html)
- Health Goods (www.healthgoods.com) – Shower Curtains
- It's a Soy Candles (www.Itsasoy.com)
- Klean Kanteen (www.kleankanteen.com)
- Luxe Candles (www.Luxecandles.com)
- Sigg (www.mysigg.com)
- Nubious Organics (www.Nubiousorganics.com)
- Real Goods (www.realgoods.com) – Cork bath mat
- Reusable Bags (www.Resusablebags.com)
- Salt Lamps (www.thesaltoftheearth.com) and (www.mysaltlamp.com) – These are supposed to improve the air we breathe. I recommend you put one next to your bed and next to your computer.
- Something Wicked Candles (www.somethingwickedcandles.com)
- Two Flush water saving toilets (www.TwoFlush.com)

For your Pleasure – Green Toys

- Babeland (www.babeland) – Check out the Eco-Sexy Kit and Eco-Delight. They also have their own line or organic lube as well as toys made from wood, stainless steal and glass.
- Earth Erotics (www.eartherotics.com) – This is a great website. They have eco-friendly sex toys for everyone. Have you ever heard of Tupperware parties? Earth Erotics has a version of that. If you are enterprising, you could be very successful.
- Egyptian Magic (www.egyptianmagic.com) – Natural lube made from honey and beeswax
- Outrageous Toys (www.amazon.com) – Try the Passion Produce line. They are phthalate-free.

- The Sensual Vegan (www.thesensualvegan.com) – These products are not tested on animals and do not contain animal ingredients. They donate 5% of all sales to **Scarleteen**, a sex-positive sex education resource site aimed at young people.

Burials and Caskets (Morbid, I know, but you can green this!)

- Casket Furniture (www.casketfurniture.com)
- Eco Casket (www.environmentalcaskets.com)
- Memorial Ecosystems, Inc. (www.memorialecosystems.com)
- Woodland Caskets in the USA (www.kentcasket.com)

Green Building

Flooring

- Armstrong (www.armstrong.com)
- Beaulieu of America (www.beaulieu-usa.com)
- Building Green (www.buildinggreen.com/products/cork) – Cork.
- Campbell and Sons (www.colcam.com)
- Carpet America Recovery Effort (www.carpetrecovery.org)
- Earth Weave Carpet Mills (www.earthweave.com)
- Environmental Bamboo Foundation (www.bamboocentral.org) – Bamboo.
- FLOR (www.florcatalog.com)
- Forest Stewardship Council (www.fscus.org) – Wood.
- Green Home (www.greenhome.com)
- Mannington (www.mannington.com)
- Rivanna Natural Designs (www.rivannadesigns.com)

Water Filtration

- Best Filters (www.bestfilters.com)
- Best Water Filters (www.thebestwaterfilters.com)
- H2O Warehouse (www.h2owarehouse.com)
- The Consumer Search Web site (www.consumersearch.net)
- The Gaiam catalog (www.gaiam)
- Water Filter Comparisons (www.waterfiltercomparisons.net)

Low or No VOC Paint

- Eco Spec by Benjamin Moore (www.benjaminmoore.com)
- Ecological Paint by Innovative Formulations (www.innovativeformulations.com)
- Safecoat by American Formulating and Manufacturing (www.afmsafecoat.com)

Insulation

- Bonded Logic (www.bondedlogic.com) - Recycled denim insulation.
- Concrete Blond's (www.formsquare.com) - Customized Insulation Panels.
- Excel Fibre (www.excelfibre.com/building/products3.html#top) - Recycled paper insulation.
- Hamilton Manufacturing Incorporated (www.hmi-mfg.com/insulation)
- HempFlax insulation (www.hempflax)

Green Roofs

- Armstrong ceiling materials (www.armstrong.com)

- Green roof by Wikipedia(http://en.wikipedia)
- Green Roofs for Healthy Cities (www.greenroofs.org)
- Green Roofs U.S. EPA
        (www.epa.gov/hiri/strategies/greenroofs.html)
- GreenGrid (www.greengridroofs.com)
- Greenroofs.com: The Resource Portal for Green Roofs
        (www.greenroofs.com)
- Institute for Research in Construction (http://irc.nrc-cnrc.gc.ca)

CFL Lighting

- Compact fluorescent lamp by Wikipedia (http://en.wikipedia)
- Focus on Energy
        (www.focusonenergy.com/Residential/Lighting/cfls)
- GE (www.GElighting.com)

LED Lighting

- Energy-Efficient Lighting
        (www.eartheasy.com/live_energyeff_lighting)
- LED Light Bulbs (www.ccrane.com/lights/led-light-bulbs/index.aspx)
- Light-emitting diode by Wikipedia (http://en.wikipedia)
- The LED Light (www.theledlight.com)

Footprint Calculators

- Carbon Calculator (www.americanforests.org)
- Carbon Footprint (www.carbonfund.org)
- Ecological Footprint (www.myfootprint.org)
- Energy Calculators
        (www.eere.energy.gov/consumer/calculators)

Water

- Water Use It Wisely (www.wateruseitwisely.com)
- Water-Savings Tips (www.h20use.net)
- WaterSense (www.epa.gov/watersense)

Energy

- Alliance to Save Energy (www.ase.org/consumers)
- Energy Savers (www.energysavers.gov)
- Energy Star (www.energystar)
- Green-e Renewable Energy Certification (www.gree-e.org)
- The Power is in Your Hands (www.powerisinyourhands.org)
- U.S. Dept. of Energy, Office of Energy Efficiency and Renewable Energy (www.eere.energy.gov)

Home and Garden

- Coalition Against the Misuse of Pesticides (www.beyondpesticides.org)
- Eco-Friendly Paints (www.eartheasy.com)
- EPA, Indigenous Plants Landscaping (www.epa.gov/greenacres)
- Gardener's Supply (www.gardeners.com)
- Gardens Alive! (www.gardensalive.com)
- USDA, Home Conservation Advice (www.nrcs.usda)

New Homes

- Build-e, Eco-Friendly Houses (www.build-e.com)
- Certified Forests Products Council (www.certifiedwood.org)
- Environmental Home Center (www.environmentalhomecenter.com)
- Environmentally Construction Outfitters (www.environproducts.com)

- No. American Insulation Manuf.'s Assoc. (www.naima.org)
- U.S. Green Building Council (www.usgbc.org)

Safety

- Environmental Protection Agency (www.epa.gov)
- Environmental Working Group (www.ewg)
- Information on Phthalates (www.mindfully.org/Plastic/Plasticizers/About-Phthalates.htm)
- PVC Dangers (www.checnet.org/healthehouse/education/articles-detail.asp?Main_ID=185)
- Teens for Safe Cosmetics (www.teens4sc.org)
- U.S. Consumer Product Safety Commission (www.cpsc.gov)

Pets

- Animal Welfare Institute (www.animalwelfareapproved.org) – Read up on the new certification for humane animal treatment.
- Bone to Pick (www.bonetopick.com)
- Ecoanimal (www.ecoanimal.com)
- Green Kitty (www.greenkitty.com)
- Heidi's Homemade Bakery (www.heidishomemadebakery.com)
- Holistic Family and Pets (www.holisticfamilyandpets.com)
- Only Natural Pet (www.onlynaturalpet.com)
- Poop Bags (www.poopbags.com)
- Sckoon Organics (www.sckoonorganics.com) – Dog Clothes.
- Sixwise (shop.sixwise.com) – Flea 'n Tick B Gone.
- Skooper Box (www.skooperbox.com)

Babes with Babies

Baby Clothes

- Better for Babies (www.Betterforbabies.com)
- Cozy Cocoon (www.cozycocoon.com)
- Ecotopia (www.Ecotopia.co.uk)
- FreeCycle (www.Freecycle.org)
- Great Green Baby (www.Greatgreenbaby.com)
- Green Babies (www.greenbabies.com)
- Lapsaky organic clothing (www.lapsaky.com)
- Maggie's Functional Organics (www.maggiesorganics.com)
- NuiOrganics (www.Nuiorganics.com)
- Pristine Planet (www.Pristineplanet.com)
- Rawganique (www.rawganique.com) – Organic Hemp Clothes.
- Restitch (www.Restitch.co.uk/)
- The Gaiam catalog (www.gaiam)
- The Natural Store (www.Thenaturalstore.co.uk)
- Under the Nile (www.underthenile.com)

Bath and Body products for baby

*Approved by organicconsumers.org.

- *Dr. Bronner's (www.drbronner) - 100% USDA organic, animal friendly, and Fair Trade. Their castile soap has 18 uses. You can use it from body soap, toothpaste, shampoo, to counter cleaner and laundry soap! It's all safe.
- *Grateful Body (www.gratefulbody.com) - Also sells a line of products for mature women.
- *Organic Essence (www.organic-essence.com) - This is one of the few companies we know where the entire product line is USDA Organic.
- *Sensibility Soaps (www.sensibilitysoaps.com)

- *Terressentials (www.terressentials)
- *Trillium Organics (www.trilliumorganics.com)
- *Vermont Soap (www.vermontsoap.com)
- Aubrey Organics (www.aubrey-organics.com)
- Avalon Organics (www.avalonorganics.com)
- Erbaviva (www.erbaviva.com)
- Jason (www.jason-natural.com)
- Little Twig (www.littletwig.com) – Donates to a children's charity.
- Munchskins – (www.baby-skin-care.info)
- Natures Gate (www.natures-gate.com)
- Pharmacopia (www.pharmacopia.net)
- Sage Baby (www.Sagebabynyc.com)
- Weleda (www.usa.weleda)

Sun Protection

- All Terrain (www.allterrainco.com)
- Aubrey Organics Natural Sun Green Tea Protective Sunscreen, SPF 25 (www.aubrey-organics.com)
- California Baby Everyday/Year-Round Moisturizing Sunscreen Lotion, SPF 18 (www.californiababy.com)
- Erbaviva Children's Sunscreen, SPF 15 (www.erbaviva.com)
- Kiss My Face Sunspray Lotion, SPF 30 (www.kissmyface.com)
- Weleda Children's Sunscreen, SPF 18+ (www.usa.weleda)

Cloth Diapers

- A Baby Connection (www.Ababyconnection.com)
- An Eco-Babe Business (www.Babybearbums.etsy.com) - Victoria Sheahan @ Queen Creek, AZ; Stay-at-home mom of 4 precious blessings.
- BacOut (http://www.bi-o-kleen.com/general.htm)
- Bummis (www.Bummis.com)

- Cloth Babies (www.Clothbabies.com)
- Cloth Diaper (www.clothdiaper.com)
- Cooperative WAHM store (www.hyenacart) – Matt and Tiffany Nixon
- Diaper Cuts(www.Diapercuts.com)
- G Diapers (www.gdiapers.com) – Flushable diapers.
- GoGo Natural (www.Gogonatural.com)
- Hyena Cart (www.HyenaCart.com) – Search cloth diapers.
- Kushies (www.kushies.com)
- Nature's Nappies (www.Naturesnappies.com)
- Our artisan shops (www.hyenacart)
- Seventh Generation (www.seventhgeneration.com) – Try their biodegradable wipes.
- The WAHM Mall (www.Thewahmmall.com) - A resource for Work At Home Mom companies. Check out the Cloth Diapering Directory.
- Tushies (www.tushies.com)
- Wild Flower Diapers (www.WildFlowerDiapers.com)

Food

- Better for Babies (www.Betterforbabies.com)
- Earth's Best (www.earthsbest.com)
- Happybaby (www.happybabyfood.com)
- Homemade Baby (www.homemadebaby.com)
- Nature's One (www.Naturesone.com)
- Plum Organics (www.plumorganics.com)
- Sweetpea Baby Food (www.sweetpeababyfood.com)
- Ulula (www.Ulula.co.uk)

Organic Formula

- Born Free BPA free plastic bottles (www.newbornfree.com)
- Earth's Best Organic Infant Formula (www.babyorganic.com)
- Nature's One Baby's Only Organic (www.naturesone.com)

- Similac Organic (www.similacorganic.com)
- Ultra Bright Beginnings Organic
  (www.brightbeginnings.com/products/organic-baby-formula.asp)

Teething

- Nova Natural Toys teething necklace (www.novanatural.com)
- Under the Nile organic cotton bumblebee teething ring
  (www.hazelnutkids.com)

Furniture

- A Natural Home (www.anaturalhome.com)
- Branch Home (www.Branchhome.com)
- EcoBedroom (www.ecobedroom.com)
- EcoChoices (www.ecochoices.com)
- Freecycle (www.Freecycle.org)
- Mothercare (www.Mothercare.com)
- Nursery Works (www.Nurseryworks.net)
- Pristine Planet (www.Pristineplanet.com)
- Vivavi (www.Vivavi.com)

Pregnancy and Mother's Needs

- Better for Babies (www.Betterforbabies.com)
- Earth Mama Angel Baby (www.Earthmamaangelbaby.com)
- Happy Healthy Baby (www.Happyhealthybaby.com)
- LunaPads (www.Lunapads.com)
- Mama Goddess (www.Mamagoddess.com)
- MotherCare (www.Mothercare.com)
- One Hot Mama (www.onehotmoma.com)

Slings, Pouches and Carriers

- Better for Babies (www.Betterforbabies.com)
- Freecycle (www.Freecycle.org)
- Natural Parenting (www.Naturalparenting.co.nz)
- Pristine Planet (www.Pristineplanet.com)
- The Sling Station (www.theslingstation.com)
- Zolowear (www.Zolowear.com)

Toys

- Baby Bunz & Co. (www.babybunz.com)
- Baby Mine Store (www.BabyMineStore.com)
- Betther for Babies (www.Betterforbabies.com)
- Branch Home (www.Branchhome.com)
- Brio (http://brio.knex:com)
- Ecotopia (www.Ecotopia.co.uk)
- Guidecraft (www.guidecraft.com)
- Hazelnut Kids (www.hazelnutkids.com)
- HearthSong (www.hearthsong.com)
- Hugg-A-Planet (www.peacetoys.com)
- Hyena Cart (www.Hyenacart.com/annemozeallwoodtoys/)
- Island Treasure Toys (www.islandtreasuretoys.com)
- Lakeshore Learning Store (www.lakeshorelearning.com)
- Lego (www.lego.com)
- Little Tikes (www.littletikes.com)
- lmaginarium Toys (www.imaginarium.com) - A division of Toys "R" Us.
- Magic Cabin (www.magiccabin.com)
- Mercurius (www.mercurius-usa.com)
- Natural Play (www.NaturaIPlay.com)
- North Star Toys (www.northstartoys.com)
- Nova Natural Toys and Crafts (www.novanatural.com)
- Our Green House (www.Ourgreenhouse.com)

- Plan Toys (www.plantoys.com)
- Play Store Toys (www.Playstoretoys.com)
- Primetime Playthings (www.intplay.com)
- Sassy (www.sassybaby.com)
- Three Sisters Toys (www.threesisterstoys.com)
- Tiny Birds Organics (www.Tinybirdsorganics.com)
- Tiny Love (www.tinylove.com)
- Willow tree Toys (www.willowtreetoys.com)

For the Kids

- Bobbie Big Foot (www.kidsfootprint.org)
- Cool Kids for A Cool Climate
        (www.coolkidsforacoolclimate.com)
- Earth Kids 911 (www.earthkids911.org)
- Green School Green Squad (www.nrdc.org/greensquad)
- Green School Project (www.greenschoolproject.com)
- Preschool and up (www.kidsplanet.org)
- Second Graders and up (www.kidsregen.org)
- Water Use Calculator
        (www.ga.water.usgs.gov/edu/sq3.html)

Natural Birthing

- American College of Nurse-Midwives
        (www.midwife.org/find.cfm)
- Birthing from Within (www.birthingfromwithin.com)
- Bradley Method (www.bradleybirth.com)
- Dona international (www.dona.org)
- The Calm Birth (www.calmbirth.org)

Babes at Work

Directory Services

- EnviroLink Network (www.envirolink.org)
- Green Living Source for the Consumer
    (www.thegreenguide.com)
- Green Pages Co-op (www.greenpages.org)
- National Environmental Directory
    (www.environmentaldirectory.net)

At Work

- Computer Recycling (www.computerrecyclingdirectory.com)
- Conservatree (www.conservatree.com)
- Greenprint (www.Printgreener.com) - Greenprint software
    (Windows) gets rid of dead pages before the printer
    has to spit them out.
- Office Footprint Calculator (www.thegreenoffice.com)
- Reducing Office Waste
    (www.filebankinc.com/reports/reduction_tips)
- Reduce.Org (www.reduce.org)
- The Real Earth, Inc. (www.treeco.com)
- Waterless Printing Association (www.Waterless.org)

Environmental Labeling

- Ecolabels (www.eco-labels)
- Electronic Product Environmental and Assessment Tool
    (www.epeat.net)
- Energy-Star® Rating System (www.energystar)
- Global Ecolabeling Network (www.gen.gr.jp)
- Green Seal Certified Cleaning Products and Paper Products
    (www.greenseal.org)

- NSF International (www.nsf.org) - Certification System.
- Transfair USA (www.transfairusa.org)

Local Recycling

- Ecocycle (www.ecocycle.org)
- Freecycle (www.freecycle.org)
- Nationwide Local Recycling Programs (www.earth911.org)
- NSF's Recycling Guide (www.nsf.org/consumer/recycling)
- Zero Waste America (www.zerowasteamerica.org)

Computer Recycling

- Earth 911 (www.earth911.org)
- Electronics Industries Alliance (www.eiae.org)

Phone Recycling

- Collective Good International (www.collectivegood.com)
- The Charitable Recycling Program
        (www.charitablerecycling.com)
- ReCellular (www.recellular.com)
- Wireless recycling (www.wirelessrecycling.com)
- Wireless Foundation (www.wirelessfoundation.org)

Supplies and Furniture

- Suppliers of Recycled Content Products
        (www.epa.gov/epaoswer/non-
        hw/procure/database.htm)
- All Steel Office (www.Allsteeloffice.com/ahrend) - Eco-
        friendly office furniture.
- Auspen (www.Auspen.com) - Refillable white board markers &
        inks.

- Be True Green (www.Betruegreen.com)
- EcoWork (www.Ecowork.com) - Eco-friendly office furniture.
- Forest Choice (www.Forestchoice.com) - Pencils from certified-sustainable cedar.
- Geami (www.Geami.com) - Eco-friendly packing and shipping materials.
- Green Earth Office Supply (www.greenearthofficesupply.com)
- Herman Miller (www.Hermanmiller.com) - Herman Miller's Mirra Chair and others are also C2C certified. The Leaf from Herman Miller is a high-end LED Desk lamp.
- Krug (www.Krug.com) - Produces office furniture with extensive ecological performance aspects.
- Legare Furniture (www.Legarefurniture.com) - Office furniture made with sustainable materials.
- Motherboard Gifts (www.Motherboardgifts.com) - Motherboard is a company that uses reclaimed circuit boards for all sorts of office and school-related products.
- Remarkable Recycled (www.Remarkable.co.uk) – Remarkable Recycled Promotional Products.
- Springbrain (www.Springbrain.com) - Springbrain office systems come in bamboo and other sustainable materials.
- Steelcase (www.Steelcase.com/na) - Office dividers from Steelcase that contain no PVC and are recyclable. The Think Chair from Steelcase.
- The Green Office (www.Thegreenoffice.com) - The Green Office is a site full of eco-office supplies from stationary to toner to cleaning products to furniture.
- Wilkhahn (www.Wilkhahn.com) - Office furniture.

Paper

- Acorn Designs (www.acorndesigns.org)
- Elephant Dung Paper (www.elephantdungpaper.com) – Paper made from recycled dung.
- Great Elephant Poo Poo Paper Company (www.poopoopaper.com) – Paper made from recycled dung.
- GreenLine Paper Company (www.greenlinepaper.com)
- Paper Organics (www.paperorganics.com)
- Sheep Poop Paper (www.creativepaperwales.co.uk) – Paper made from recycled dung.
- Treecycle (www.Treecycle.com) - Treecycle Recycled Paper.
- Twisted Limb Paper (www.twistedlimbpaper.com)

Investment

- First Affirmative Financial Network (www.firstaffirmative.com)
- Grarneen (www.grameen-info.org)
- Progressive Asset Management (www.progressive-asset.com)
- Social Funds/SRI World Group, Inc. (www.socialfunds.com)
- Social Investment Forum (www.socialinvest.org)

General Green Resources

Food

- CSA (www.csacenter.org)
- Diamond Organics (www.diamondorganics.com)
- Eartheasy (www.eartheasy.com)
- Equal Exchange (www.equalexchange.com)
- EV Living (www.Evliving.com)
- Fresh Direct (www.freshdirect.com)

- Green Feet
  (www.Greenfeet.net/newsletter/eatorganic.shtml)
- Green People (www.Greenpeople.org/HomeDelivery.html) -
  Co-op and buying club directory
- Green Restaurant Association (www.dinegreen.com)
- Listing of Farmers markets (www.ams.usda)
- Local Harvest (www.localharvest.org)
- Organic Consumers
  (www.Organicconsumers.org/organic/natfrugal012306.cfm
)
- Organic Consumers Buying Guide
  (www.Organicconsumers.org/btc/BuyingGuide.cfm)
- Planet Friendly (www.Planetfriendly.net/organic.html)
- Seafood Choices Alliance (www.seafoodchoices.com)
- SLOW Food International (www.slowfood.com)
- SPUD (www.spud.com) – Small Potatoes Urban Delivery
- Trader Joe's (www.traderjoes.com)
- TransFair USA (www.transfairusa.org)
- U.S. Dept of Agriculture National Organic Program
  (www.ams.usda
- U.S. Dept of Agriculture Nutrition Information
  (www.nutrition.gov)
- Whole Foods Market (www.wholefoods.com)

Shopping

- Coalition for Consumer Information on Cosmetics
  (www.leapingbunny.org)
- Consumer Reports (www.consumerreports.org)
- Co-op America, National Green Pages
  (www.coopamerica.org/pubs/greenpages/)
- Earth Animal (www.earthanimal.com)
- Ecomall-Environmental Shopping Center (www.ecomall.com)

- Global Exchange/Fair Trade (www.globalexchange.org)
- Green Living Now (www.greenlivingnow.com)
- My Gift List (www.mygiftlist.com) – Make your own eco-friendly gift registry
- One Percent for the Planet (www.onepercentfortheplanet.org)
- Professional Wet-cleaning Network (www.tpwn.net)
- Responsible Shopper (www.responsibleshopper.org)
- Reusable Shopping Bags (www.reuseablebags.com)
- The Animal Rescue Site (www.theanimalrescuesite.com) – Shop where a portion of your money will help shelter animals.
- The World Wildlife Fund Shop (www.worldwildlife.org)

Transport

- Center for Climate Change & Environmental Forecasting (www.climate.dot.gov)
- Car Information-Mileage, Hybrids (www.fueleconomy)
- Electric Bikes (www.electric-bikes.com)
- Electric Vehicle Assoc. of America (www.evaa.org)
- Environmental Guide to Cars and Trucks (www.greenercars.com)
- EV Rental Cars (www.everental.com)
- Flex Car (www.flexcar.com)
- Hopstop (www.hopstop.com) – Information about public transportation
- Transportation Almanac-Energy, Pollution (www.bicycleuniverse.info)
- Travel Green (www.travel-green.org)
- U.S. Council for Automotive Research (www.uscar.org)

Sustainable Lifestyles

- American Forests (www.americanforests.org)

- Conservatree (www.conservatree.org)
- Earth Easy (www.eartheasy.com)
- Earth 911 (www.earth911.org)
- Forest Stewardship Council (www.fsc.org)
- Green Globe (www.greenglobe21.com)
- National Arbor Day Foundation (www.arborday.org)
- National Parks Conservation Association (www.npca.org)
- Trees for the Future (www.treesftf.org)
- U.S. Green Building Council (www.usbg.org)

Advocacy Groups and Organizations

- American Council for An Energy-Efficient Economy (www.aceee.org)
- Blue Ocean Institute (www.blueocean.org)
- Certified Humane (www.certifiedhumane.com)
- Children's Health Environmental Coalition (www.checnet.org)
- Earthshare (www.earthshare.org)
- Environmental Defense Fund (www.environmentaldefense.org)
- Environmental Protection Agency (www.epa.gov)
- Environmental Working Group (www.ewg)
- Friends of the Earth (www.foe.org)
- Green Peace USA (www.greenpeace.org)
- Idealist (www.idealist.org)
- Marine Stewardship Council (www.msc.org)
- Natural Resources Defense Council (www.nrdc)
- Rainforest Action Network (www.ran.org)
- Redefining Progress (www.rprogress.org)
- Rocky Mountain Institute (www.rmi.org)
- Social Marketing Institute (www.social-marketing.org/index.html)
- Stop Global Warming (www.stopglobalwarming.org)
- The Conservation Fund (www.conservationfund.org)

- The Nature Conservancy (www.nature.org)
- The Ocean Conservancy (www.oceanconservancy.org)
- Worldwatch Institute (www.worldwatch.org)
- World Resources Institute (www.wri.org)
- World Wildlife Fund (www.wwf.org)

Media

- E/The Environmental Magazine (www.emagazine.com)
- Earth Policy Institute (www.earth-policy.org)
- Environmental Issues Newsletter
(www.environment.about.com)
- Environmental Health News
(www.environmentalhealthnews.org)
- Environmental News Network (www.enn.com)
- Grist Magazine (www.grist.org)
- Tree Hugger (www.treehugger.com) – Online Magazine.

Government Agencies

- EPA Climate Leaders (www.epa.gov/climateleaders)
- Materials Exchange Resources
(www.epa.gov/jtr/comm/exchange.htm)
- U.S. Environmental Protection Agency, Energy Star Program
(www.energystar)
- U.S. Environmental Protection Agency, Waste Wise Program
(www.epa.gov/epaoswer/non-hw/reduce/wstewise)
- USDA National Organic Program (www.ams.usda)
- WaterSense (www.epa.gov/watersense)

Greenhouse gases

- Greenhouse Gas Protocol (www.ghgprotocol.org)

- The Climate Trust (www.climatetrust.org)

Carbon offsetters

- American Solar Energy Society (www.ases.org)
- American Wind Energy Association (www.awea.org)
- Atmosfair (www.atmosfair.com) – Invest in solar power for developing countries.
- Carbonfund (www.carbonfund.org)
- Climate Counts (www.climatecounts.org) – See how major companies offset their carbon emissions.
- Climate Friendly (www.climatefriendly.com) – Invest in renewable energy in Australia and New Zealand.
- Flex Your Power (www.fypower.org/)
- Guide to Buying Clean Energy (www.nrdc.org/air/energy/gcleanen.asp)
- My Climate (www.myclimate.org) – Invest in greenhouse, farms, and biomass facilities.
- Native Energy (www.nativeenergy.com) – Calculate your carbon footprint and invest in offsets of wind-power and methane-gas energy.
- Pick Your Power (www.green-e.org/your_e_choices/pyp.html)

Index

C

References

[1] Interesting article on this at
http://www.westland.net/Venice/art/cronk/consumer.htm
[2] The Power and the Promise of Ecological Feminism by Karen Warren
[3] (FDA) Food and Drug Administration. (1999). *Tampons and asbestos, dioxin, and toxic shock syndrome.* Retrieved February 2, 2008 from http://www.fda.gov/cdrh/consumer/tamponsabs.pdf

Armstrong, l., & Scott, A. (1992). *Whitewash: Exposing the Health and Environmental Dangers of Women's Sanitary Products and Disposable Diapers – What You Can Do About It!* New York: Harper Perennial.

Houppert, K. (1999). *The Curse – Menstruation: Confronting the Last Unmentionable Taboo. New* York: Farrar, Straus, & Giroux.

[4] http://www.emedicinehealth.com/toxic_shock_syndrome/article_em.htm

[5] http://www.4woman.gov/faq/endomet.htm

[6] Bobel, C. (2006). "Our revolution has style": Contemporary menstrual product activists "doing feminism: in the third wave. *Sex Roles, 54 (5/6),* 331-345.

[7] Tierno, P., & Hanna, B. (1989). Ecology of toxic shock syndrome: Amplification of toxic shock syndrome toxin 1 by materials of medical interest. *Review of Infectious diseases, 11 (Suppl1),* S182-6-S186-7.

[8] (SEAC) Student Environmental Action Coalition. (n.d.). *TampAction.* Retrieved February 3, 2008 from http://www.seac

Wilkins, E. (2000). *Pull the Plug on the Feminine Hygiene Industry.* Self-published zine.

Bobel, C. (2006). "Our revolution has style": Contemporary menstrual product activists "doing feminism: in the third wave. *Sex Roles, 54 (5/6),* 331-345.

[9] (SEAC) Student Environmental Action Coalition. (n.d.). *TampAction.* Retrieved February 3, 2008 from http://www.seac

[10] (SEAC) Student Environmental Action Coalition. (n.d.). *TampAction*. Retrieved February 3, 2008 from http://www.seac

[11] (SEAC) Student Environmental Action Coalition. (n.d.). *TampAction*. Retrieved February 3, 2008 from http://www.seac

[12] Bobel, C. (2006). "Our revolution has style": Contemporary menstrual product activists "doing feminism: in the third wave. *Sex Roles, 54 (5/6),* 331-345.

Wilkins, E. (2000). *Pull the Plug on the Feminine Hygiene Industry*. Self-published zine.

[13] Charlesworth, D. (2001). Paradoxical constructions of self: Educating young women about menstruation. *Woman and Language, 24 (2),* 13-20.

Connelly, P. (2007). Fresh, clean – and hidden. Women's Review of Books, *24 (4),* 18-19.

[14] Bobel, C. (2006). "Our revolution has style": Contemporary menstrual product activists "doing feminism: in the third wave. *Sex Roles, 54 (5/6),* 331-345.

Wilkins, E. (2000). *Pull the Plug on the Feminine Hygiene Industry*. Self-published zine.

[15] Erchul, M. J., Chrisler, J. C., Gorman, J. A., & Johnston-Robledo, I. (2002). Education and advertising: A content analysis of commercially produced booklets about menstruation. *Journal of Early adolescence, 22,* 455-475.

[16] Images used in this chapter are from lunapads.com.

[17] Reprinted with permission from the Lunapads.com website

[18] http://www.safecosmetics.org/newsroom/nyt_2_15_07.cfm

[19] http://www.ewg.org/node/21286

[20] http://www.ewg.org/node/17964

[21] http://www.cosmeticsdatabase.com/research/whythismatters.php

[22] http://www.fda.gov/FDAC/features/1998/398_cosm.html

[23] For more information visit organicconsumers.org.

[24] www.drbronner.com

[25] Based on http://www.thedailygreen.com/healthy-eating-plans/

[26] http://www.evliving.com/2008/07/08/814/environmental-consequences-livestock/

[27] U.S. Department of Labor 2000 Southern California Garment Compliance Survey Fact Sheet, August 2000.

[28] O'Rourke, Dara. "Sweatshops 101: Lessons in Monitoring Apparel Production Around the World". *Dollars & Sense*, Issue #237, Sept/Oct 2001.

[29] "The WWD List, The Big Boys, The 20 U.S. apparel executives at publicly listed companies with the highest compensation packages in 2002," Women's Wear Daily, July 10, 2003.

[30] Based on a 40-hour workweek and 52 weeks of work per year.

[31] International Labor Organization.

[32] Enloe, Cynthia. "The Globetrotting Sneaker". *Ms. Magazine*, Sept/Oct 1995.

[33] Enloe, Cynthia. "The Globetrotting Sneaker". Ms. Magazine (Sept/Oct 1995)

[34] The numbers and facts in *Deadly Cotton* are from the World Health Organization, United Nations Food and Agriculture Organization, and United Nations Environment Programme.

[35] Environmental Justice Foundation. "The Deadly Chemicals in Cotton". ejfoundation.org/pdf/the_deadly_chemicals_in_cotton.pdf

[36] Environmental Justice Foundation "White Gold, The True Cost of Cotton: Uzbekistan, Cotton and the Crushing of a Nation" http://www.ejfoundation.org/pdf/white_gold_the_true_cost_of_cotton.pdf

[37] www.seventhgeneration.com

[38] http://www.reuters.com/article/pressRelease/idUS219256+23-Sep-2008+PRN20080923

[39] http://www.ameriflowrecycling.com/recycling_facts

[40] The pictures in this section are from nubiousorganics.com.

[41] Hormone mimics hit home. Consumer Reports. June 1998;63(6):52.

[42] Check out http://www.care2.com/greenliving/kitchen-plastic-easy-greening.html for more information about plastics.

[43]http://naturalhealthcare.ca/herbology_101.phtml?d=y&herb=Pennyroy al

[44] Armstrong, l., & Scott, A. (1992). Whitewash: Exposing the Health and Environmental Dangers of Women's Sanitary Products and Disposable Diapers – What You Can Do About It! New York: Harper Perennial.

[45] Allsopp, Michelle. Achieving Zero Dioxin: An emergency strategy for dioxin elimination. September 1994. Greenpeace. http://archive.greenpeace.org/toxics/reports/azd/azd.html

[46] Greenpeace. New Tests Confirm TBT Poison in Procter & Gamble's Pampers: Greenpeace Demands World-Wide Ban of Organotins in All Products. 15 May 2000. http://archive.greenpeace.org/pressreleases/toxics/2000may 152.html

[47] Partsch, C.J., Aukamp, M., and Sippell, W.G. Scrotal temperature is increased in disposable plastic lined nappies. Division of Paediatric Endocrinology, Department of Paediatrics, Christian-Albrechts- University of Kiel, Schwanenweg 20, D-24105 Kiel, Germany. Arch Dis Child 2000;83:364-368.

[48] Weiner, F. 1979. The relationship of diapers to diaper rashes in the one-month-old infant. The Journal of Pediatrics, 95: 422-424.

[49] Lehrburger, Carl. 1988. Diapers in the Waste Stream: A review of waste management and public policy issues. 1988. Sheffield, MA: self-published.

[50] Lehrburger, C., J. Mullen and C.V. Jones. 1991. Diapers: Environmental Impacts and Lifecycle Analysis. Philadelphia, PA: Report to The National Association of Diaper Services (NADS).

[51] Link, Ann. Disposable nappies: a case study in waste prevention. April 2003. Women's Environmental Network.

[52] Link, Ann. Disposable nappies: a case study in waste prevention. April 2003. Women's Environmental Network.

[53] Stone, Janis and Sternweis, Laura. Consumer Choice -- Diaper Dilemma. Iowa Sate University - University Extension. ID.# 1401. 1994. http://www.rockwellcollins.com/daycare/pdf/pm1401.pdf

[54] Realdiaperassociation.org – Real Diaper Association

[55] Percent of People in Poverty by Definition of Income and Selected Characteristics: 2002 (Revised). http://www.census.gov/hhes/poverty/poverty02/r&dtable5.html

[56] McKay, Kim. & Bennin, Jenny. (2008) True Green @ Work; 100 ways you can make the environment your business.

Made in the USA
Lexington, KY
03 March 2010